A CHILD'S INTRODUCTION TO
Egyptology

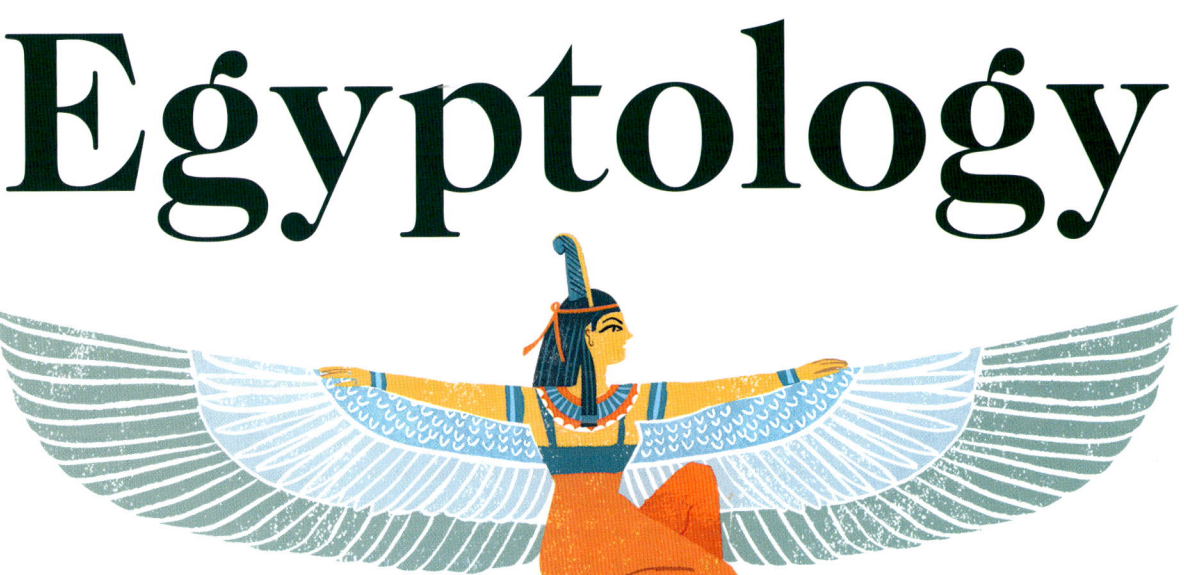

A CHILD'S INTRODUCTION TO
Egyptology

The Mummies, Pyramids, Pharaohs, Gods, and Goddesses of Ancient Egypt

HEATHER ALEXANDER

Illustrated by SARA MULVANNY

BLACK DOG
& LEVENTHAL
PUBLISHERS
NEW YORK

Black Dog & Leventhal Publishers
Hachette Book Group
1290 Avenue of the Americas
New York, NY 10104

www.hachettebookgroup.com
www.blackdogandleventhal.com

First Edition: March 2021

Black Dog & Leventhal Publishers is an imprint of Perseus Books, LLC, a subsidiary of Hachette Book Group, Inc. The Black Dog & Leventhal Publishers name and logo are trademarks of Hachette Book Group, Inc.

The publisher is not responsible for websites (or their content) that are not owned by the publisher.

The Hachette Speakers Bureau provides a wide range of authors for speaking events. To find out more, go to www.HachetteSpeakersBureau.com or call (866) 376-6591.

Print book interior design by Katie Benezra

Image credits: desifoto (Getty Images 1065390466); tanys04 (Getty Images 1130326109); oleksii arseniuk (Getty Images 1161616299); SpicyTruffel (Getty Images 1140277566); Anatolii Kovalov (Getty Images 1148379401)

Library of Congress Cataloging-in-Publication Data
Names: Alexander, Heather, 1967- author. | Mulvanny, Sara, illustrator.
Title: A child's introduction to Egyptology : the mummies, pyramids, pharaohs, gods, and goddesses /
Heather Alexander ; illustrated by Sara Mulvanny
Description: First edition. | New York : Black Dog & Leventhal Publishers, 2021. | Includes index. | Audience: Ages 8-11 |
Summary: "A charmingly illustrated exploration of the wonders of Ancient Egypt—from pyramids and mummies to pharaohs and god—for curious kids ages 8 to 11 to enjoy"—Provided by publisher.
Identifiers: LCCN 2020016100 (print) | LCCN 2020016101 (ebook) |
ISBN 9780762471577 (hardcover) | ISBN 9780762471584 (ebook)
Subjects: LCSH: Egypt—Civilization—Juvenile literature.
Classification: LCC DT61 .A49865 2021 (print) | LCC DT61 (ebook) | DDC 932/.01—dc23
LC record available at https://lccn.loc.gov/2020016100
LC ebook record available at https://lccn.loc.gov/2020016101

ISBNs: 978-0-7624-7157-7 (hardcover), 978-0-7624-7158-4 (ebook)

Printed in China

APS

10 9 8 7 6 5 4 3

To Joe, Liv, Phee, and Luna

Special thanks to Professor Laurel D. Bestock,
Associate Professor of Archaeology and the Ancient World and
Egyptology and Assyriology, Brown University

Special thanks to Sara Mulvanny,
whose lovely illustrations fill these pages

Contents

INTRODUCTION
ANCIENT EGYPT

HAVE YOU EVER heard of…

MUMMIES

PYRAMIDS

THE SPHINX

CLEOPATRA

KING TUT

MUMMY CURSES

HIEROGLYPHIC WRITING

They're all part of an amazing time in history and a civilization known as ancient Egypt.

EGYPT

Egypt is a country in northeast Africa. The Mediterranean Sea lies to the north, and the Red Sea lies to the east. It's a land of hot deserts, where the sun shines brightly and there's little rain and few trees. This ancient land—where the pharaohs once ruled—is the same land that modern people live on today, and it is still called Egypt.

ANCIENT

Egypt's civilization is "ancient," because it started a long, long time ago. How long? Five thousand years!

THE BEGINNING OF THE STORY

When Egypt started out, it was split into two separate regions—Upper Egypt and Lower Egypt. King Narmer (he was also called King Menes) joined them together and became the first king, or pharaoh. This began the story of ancient Egypt. The ancient Egyptians went on to create one of the most advanced and powerful civilizations. It lasted for 3,000 years, which is an extremely long time. (By comparison, the United States has only been a country for less than 250 years!) Ancient Egyptians gave the world many inventions and left behind thousands of written records, monuments, statues, and artifacts that we study and learn from today.

MEDITERRANEAN SEA

FUN FACT

An Egyptologist studies the history, art, architecture, language, and customs of ancient Egypt.

An archaeologist studies the history of human civilizations by digging up objects from the past.

LIBYA

EGYPT

RED SEA

NUBIA

LIVING IN A DESERT LAND

Ninety-seven percent of ancient Egypt's land was desert—and the scorching sand was one of the reasons the civilization survived for so long. The desert acted like a wall, protecting Egypt from invaders. Few attackers risked traveling across miles and miles of hot, empty land with nowhere to hide and nowhere to find water or shade. This built-in barrier prevented Egypt from having many wars and allowed it to grow and develop.

THE NILE RIVER

IN ADDITION TO the desert, ancient Egypt would not have succeeded without the Nile River.

SOIL SECRET

Crops need moist, fertile soil to grow. If crops can't grow, there's no food to eat. And if there's no food, people and animals don't survive. Egypt is in a huge desert, and sand is terrible for growing crops. So how did ancient Egypt become one of the most important civilizations? What was their secret for survival and success?

The Nile River! Every summer, the Nile overflowed and flooded the nearby land. The dry soil along its banks turned into thick, black mud. This rich soil was excellent for growing crops. These crops provided plenty of food to eat—and there were even leftovers to trade with other civilizations. All this food helped ancient Egypt survive and thrive for so long.

THE NILE FILE

The Nile River:

- is one of the longest rivers in the world.

- flows through the middle of Egypt—and through ten other countries in Africa.

- flows south to north.

- empties into the Mediterranean Sea. (The area where a river flows into the sea is called the "delta.")

BLACK AND RED

Ancient Egyptians called their country "Kemet," which meant "black land," because of the important black soil. They called the desert "Deshret," which meant "red land."

YOU KNOW, THE RIVER

Ancient Egyptians didn't bother naming the river. There was only one river, and it was the center of everyone's lives. They simply called it "the river." The name "Nile" came from the Greeks many years later.

RIVER SEASONS

Ancient Egyptian farmers divided the year into three seasons based on the Nile River.

• Akhet (June to September)—Nile flooded.

• Peret (October to February)—crops grew.

• Shemu (March to May)—crops were harvested.

They divided each season into four months. Each month had thirty days. Do the math: 30 × 12 = ? You get 360 days. However, the ancient Egyptians were the first to figure out that a year has 365 days (the amount of time it takes the Earth to travel around the sun), so they added five days between Shemu and Akhet and called them "the birthdays of the gods."

GIFTS FROM THE RIVER

Ancient Egyptians relied upon the river for food, clothing, building materials, supplies, transportation, drinking, and washing.

• Crops, such as wheat, barley, flax, beans, lettuce, turnips, onions, garlic, grapes, figs, dates, plums, pomegranates, and melons, were grown along the river. Flax was used to make linen cloth and rope.

• Fish were caught with nets, hooks, and harpoons.

• Dried river mud was used to make bricks to build houses.

• Tall papyrus reeds grown on the riverbanks were used to make paper, boats, shoes, and baskets.

• The river was used like a water highway, because there were no cars and few roads. Wooden boats carried people and supplies from city to city.

• People and animals drank the river's fresh water.

• People bathed and washed their clothes in the river.

How to Make Papyrus

WHAT YOU NEED

- Brown paper bag or parchment paper
- 1 cup of flour
- 2 cups of water
- Wax paper
- Aluminum foil
- Bowl
- Stirring stick
- Rolling pin
- Crayons

WHAT YOU DO

1. Cover your work area with wax paper (or parchment paper), so you don't make a mess.

2. Rip the paper bag or parchment paper into 1-inch strips of equal length.

3. In the bowl, combine the flour and the water and stir to make a glue-like mixture.

4. Dip the strips of paper into the mixture and place them horizontally side by side (overlapping slightly) on the wax paper.

5. Apply a second layer of strips vertically on top of the first layer.

6. Cover your "papyrus" with a sheet of aluminum foil. Roll over it with the rolling pin to flatten. (If you don't have a rolling pin, you can roll over it with the aluminum foil tube.)

7. Let your paper dry overnight. Make sure it is *completely* dry before lifting it. Be careful—it's very delicate!

8. Decorate your "papyrus" with crayons.

RIVER ANIMALS

Many animals lived in and along the Nile River, such as hippopotamuses, crocodiles, snakes, and geese. Ancient Egyptians feared the huge hippo with its wide mouth and sharp teeth. When threatened, it attacked boats and people along the river.

REED ALL ABOUT IT

Papyrus reeds were used to make a material that was used like paper. The inner fiber of the reeds was cut into long strips and laid in crisscross layers, one horizontal and one vertical. Then they were smashed down and dried to make scrolls of thick papyrus paper.

RELIGION, PRIESTS, AND TEMPLES

RELIGION WAS A *huge* part of the ancient Egyptians' lives. They worshipped many different gods and goddesses. There were weather gods, harvest gods, family gods, rising-and-setting-of-the-sun gods, water-flowing-on-the-Nile gods, and hundreds of others. The gods often had the heads of animals, but this didn't mean the ancient Egyptians worshipped animals. Instead they used certain animal features to symbolize the qualities of the gods.

Did the ancient Egyptians fear their gods?

Not usually. Most were friendly and were viewed with awe and wonder.

Where were the gods and goddesses worshipped?

At home and in temples.

What were the temples for?

Pharaohs built temples to worship the gods. People believed that the gods and goddesses lived inside the temples. Only the pharaoh and priests were allowed inside. Occasionally, common people were invited in for festivals.

What were the two types of temples?

There were "cult" temples that were each dedicated to one god or goddess, and there were mortuary temples that were dedicated to a pharaoh, who was worshipped there as a god when he died.

What was the largest temple?

The Temple of Karnak in Luxor. It's larger than 150 football fields put together!

What did priests do?

Priests took care of the gods—not the people, the way priests do today. They lived at the temples, and every day it was their job to feed and clothe the statues of the gods. They even bathed them and got them ready for bed! Priests also said special prayers and performed songs and dances for the gods.

What did the priests feed the statues?

The priests "fed" a god statue freshly baked bread, meat, fruit, beer, and wine three times a day. When the god was thought to be done eating, the food was taken away. Priests weren't allowed to eat anything until the god had finished his or her meal.

Why were priests obsessed with cleanliness?

Ancient Egyptians thought the gods were pure and the human world was dirty. Every day the priests washed the gods' statues, rubbed them with scented oils, dressed them in fresh linen clothes, put on sparkling gold jewelry, and applied makeup. Priests had to be pure, too. They shaved off all their body hair—even their eyebrows and eyelashes!—and washed themselves twice a day and twice a night.

GODS AND GODDESSES
A WHO'S WHO

RA —or— RE
GOD *of the* SUN

PRONUNCIATION: RAH

APPEARANCE: A man with a falcon head and a headdress with a sun disk. The sun was circled by the uraeus, a cobra that symbolized royalty. Ra's right eye represented the sun, and his left eye represented the moon.

JOBS/POWERS: Supreme ruler of all gods and the creator of all life. As the sun god, he gave light, warmth, and growth. The sun was of major importance to the ancient Egyptians, since they lived in the desert.

FAMILY CONNECTIONS: According to myths, Ra created himself from the ancient waters. Then he created Shu (air) and Tefnut (moisture), who then created Geb (Earth) and Nut (Sky). Geb and Nut gave birth to Osiris, Isis, Seth, and Nephthys. Also father of Ma'at, Sekhmet, and Bastet.

DID YOU KNOW?

● During the day, Ra sailed across the sky in a boat (symbolizing the sun). When the day ended, he sailed through the Underworld, and the moon lit the world above. In the Underworld, he had to sail his boat through twelve doors, which symbolized the twelve hours of nighttime, and fight off monsters. The next morning he'd return to the sky, victorious and reborn.

● The evil giant serpent god Apep was his greatest enemy. Apep symbolized darkness. The gods had to battle him each night so the boat/sun could rise each morning. If Apep won, the weather would be dark and stormy that day.

● Later in Egyptian history, Ra was combined with the god Amun and called Amun-Ra.

OSIRIS

GOD *of the* DEAD

PRONUNCIATION: oh-SIRE-is

APPEARANCE: A mummified man with green skin and a beard. He wore a white ostrich-feather headdress and carried a crook (a cane with a hooked handle) and a flail (a rod with three strands of beads attached to the top).

JOBS/POWERS: Ruler of the Underworld (land of the dead) and judge of the dead. He only allowed people who had lived good lives into the Underworld. He was seen as the first king of Egypt and was thought to be wise and gentle. He was also the god of agriculture and the harvest.

FAMILY CONNECTIONS: Husband of Isis, father of Horus; son of Geb and Nut; brother to Seth, Isis, and Nephthys.

DID YOU KNOW?

● Osiris was a king who died, so it was believed that pharaohs became Osiris after death.

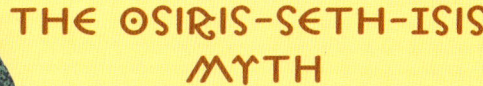

THE OSIRIS-SETH-ISIS MYTH
(or How the Underworld Began)

OSIRIS WAS CROWNED king of Egypt and his sister-wife, Isis, became queen. His evil brother, Seth, was very jealous. He wanted to rule Egypt, so he killed Osiris. Seth tore his brother's body into forty-two pieces and scattered them throughout Egypt. Then Seth declared himself king.

Isis was very upset. She traveled all over and found every body part. With the help of Seth's son, Anubis, and her sister, Nephthys, she put them back together. Then she buried her husband's body. The gods were impressed by her caring, so they brought Osiris back to life and made him Ruler of the Underworld, and his son, Horus, became king on Earth.

ISIS

GODDESS *of* MAGIC, MOTHERHOOD, *and* FAMILY LIFE

PRONUNCIATION: EYE-sis

APPEARANCE: A woman with a headdress in the shape of a throne.

JOBS/POWERS: One of the most popular gods, she protected families and helped those in need. She cast spells to fight off evil and had the power to heal. She once healed Horus from a scorpion sting.

FAMILY CONNECTIONS: Wife of Osiris, mother of Horus; daughter of Geb and Nut; sister to Osiris, Seth, and Nephthys.

DID YOU KNOW?

● Because Isis rebuilt the body of Osiris, she is associated with magical power and healing.

● When the Nile River flooded each year, ancient Egyptians said the flooding was caused by Isis crying for Osiris.

NEPHTHYS
GODDESS of DEATH

PRONUNCIATION: NEP-these

APPEARANCE: A woman in a long dress carrying a house and a basket on her head.

JOBS/POWERS: She watched over mummies, comforted the families of the dead, and helped with childbirth.

FAMILY CONNECTIONS: Daughter of Geb and Nut; sister of Isis, Osiris, and Seth; wife of Seth; mother of Anubis.

DID YOU KNOW?

- She was called upon during funerals to help the dead.

- She was the protector of the phoenix Bennu.

SETH —OR— SET

GOD of DARKNESS, STORMS, the DESERT, and DROUGHT

PRONUNCIATION: SET

APPEARANCE: The body of a human and the head of an imaginary animal similar to a fox but with rectangular ears, a long, curved snout, and a forked tail. Egyptologists call it the "Seth animal."

JOBS/POWERS: He was mean and quick to anger. He could bring about sandstorms and drought. A drought happened in Egypt when the Nile River didn't flood the nearby land, causing crops to die and people to go hungry.

FAMILY CONNECTIONS: Son of Geb and Nut; brother to Osiris, Isis, and Nephthys; husband of Nephthys; father of Anubis.

DID YOU KNOW?

● Seth defended Ra's boat against the evil serpent Apep.

● Like the desert, he is associated with the color red.

● In one version of the Osiris-Seth-Isis myth, there is a dramatic final battle between Horus and Seth. Seth takes the shape of a hippopotamus, but Horus stabs him with ten harpoons and kills him. Ancient Egyptians reenacted this story at festivals to honor Horus. In front of the crowd, the pharaoh or a priest would spear a model of a hippo. Then a cake shaped like a hippo would be cut up and the people would eat it, symbolically "destroying" Seth.

HORUS

GOD *of the* SKY

PRONUNCIATION: HOR-us

APPEARANCE: A falcon or a man with the head of a falcon and a red-and-white crown. The sun and the moon are also said to be Horus's eyes.

JOBS/POWERS: Protector of the pharaohs.

FAMILY CONNECTIONS: Son of Isis and Osiris.

EYE OF HORUS

The "Eye of Horus" is one of the most powerful Egyptian symbols. It was drawn as an eye with a curved tail, a teardrop, and an eyebrow. It was used for protection.

The myth goes like this: Horus challenged his uncle, Seth, to be king of the gods. During their battle, Seth gouged out or hurt Horus's left eye. But the god Thoth used magic to repair it. Ancient Egyptians believed this explained the different shapes of the moon, since Horus's left eye was supposed to be the moon. Horus's repaired eye saw everything and helped him ward off evil from the world.

DID YOU KNOW?

● His bitter enemy was Seth, whom he defeated to rule the world.

● He steered Ra's boat through the sky and the Underworld.

HATHOR

GODDESS *of* LOVE, MOTHERHOOD, BEAUTY, MUSIC, LAUGHTER, *and* FUN

PRONUNCIATION: HATH-or

APPEARANCE: A woman with cow horns with the sun resting between the two horns.

JOBS/POWERS: Her main job was to protect the king (her name means "House of Horus"). She also cared for all women and was called the Mother Goddess. She looked after the souls of the dead in the Underworld, giving them food from under the shade of a sycamore tree. She was also the protector of miners, keeping them safe.

FAMILY CONNECTIONS: Mother of Horus (yes, Isis is also the mother of Horus—Egyptian mythology is complicated this way!); sister to Sekhmet, Bastet, Ma'at, Shu, and Tefnut.

DID YOU KNOW?

● She rode in Horus's boat that traveled through the sky.

● She shook a sistrum, a rattle-like instrument that kept away evil.

MA'AT

GODDESS of TRUTH and JUSTICE

PRONUNCIATION: MAH-at

APPEARANCE: A goddess with wings.

JOBS/POWERS: She kept the universe in balance and judged the behavior of gods and people. She also controlled the stars and seasons.

FAMILY CONNECTIONS: Daughter of Ra; may have been married to Thoth.

DID YOU KNOW?

● The Feather of Ma'at was an ostrich feather that symbolized truth and justice. The god Anubis would place the feather of Ma'at on one side of a scale and the heart of a dead person on the other. If the heart weighed more than the feather, it meant the person had done unkind and dishonest things in life. A heart that was lighter than the feather meant the person was honest and had done many good deeds. The person with the light heart made it into the afterlife. The person with the heavy heart was devoured by the monstrous goddess Ammit (a mixture of lioness, crocodile, and hippopotamus—all man-eating animals).

ANUBIS

GOD of EMBALMING

PRONUNCIATION: a-NOO-bis

APPEARANCE: A man with a jackal head (a jackal is a wild dog); often shown in black, the color of the rich Nile soil, symbolizing rebirth.

JOBS/POWERS: He guided the dead through the Underworld and guarded the scales where the hearts of the dead were weighed. He created the first mummy from the body of Osiris.

FAMILY CONNECTIONS: Son of Nephthys and either Seth, Osiris, or Ra; brother of Horus.

DID YOU KNOW?

- When making a mummy, the head priest-embalmer wore a jackal mask to look like Anubis.

- Jackals were often found living around cemeteries.

THOTH

GOD of KNOWLEDGE, the MOON, and MAGIC

PRONUNCIATION: TOTE

APPEARANCE: A human with an ibis head. (An ibis is a long, thin bird with a curved beak.) He is sometimes shown as half human, half baboon.

JOBS/POWERS: He gave advice to the other gods and settled their arguments. Ancient Egyptians believed he wrote the Book of the Dead and created mathematics, writing, and medicine.

FAMILY CONNECTIONS: He had no parents—he created himself! Ma'at may have been his wife.

DID YOU KNOW?

- Thoth (and Ma'at) stood next to Ra on Ra's nightly boat trip across the sky.

- According to the myths, he created the 365-day calendar.

SEKHMET

GODDESS of HEALING and MEDICINE and GODDESS of WAR

PRONUNCIATION: SEK-met

APPEARANCE: The body of a woman and the head of a lioness wearing a headdress in the shape of a sun disk surrounded by a serpent. She was often in a red dress, symbolizing war and bloodshed.

JOBS/POWERS: She breathed fire (some believed the hot desert winds were her breath) and used the harmful rays of the sun's heat (as flaming arrows) to battle enemies. She could cure diseases and helped doctors, but she could also sicken those who angered her.

FAMILY CONNECTIONS: Her father was the sun god Ra, and she was created from the fire of his eye.

SOBEK

GOD of CROCODILES

PRONUNCIATION: SO-beck

APPEARANCE: A crocodile or a man with the head of a crocodile.

JOBS/POWERS: As the crocodile god, he was associated with the strength and power of the all-important Nile River. (Some believed he created the river.) He protected people from the dangers in the water. But, like a crocodile, he could sometimes be violent and unpredictable.

FAMILY CONNECTIONS: Some myths say his father was Seth, and he helped give birth to Horus.

DID YOU KNOW?

- She always went with the pharaoh into battle.

- She could be very scary!

DID YOU KNOW?

- Ancient Egyptians kept live crocodiles in temples and pools to honor Sobek.

- Thousands of mummified crocodiles have been found in tombs.

- Sobek was also god of the army, giving to them the ferocious strength of a crocodile.

TEFNUT

GODDESS of MOISTURE, RAIN, and DEW

PRONUNCIATION: TEF-noot

APPEARANCE: A lioness or a woman with the head of a lioness. Sometimes she is shown as a woman wearing on her head a solar disk circled by two cobras.

JOBS/POWERS: She helped support the sky, and each morning she caught the sun rising from the east.

FAMILY CONNECTIONS: She was the daughter of Ra, sister of Shu, and mother of Geb and Nut.

HAPY

GOD of FLOODING (or GOD of INUNDATION)

PRONUNCIATION: HAH-pee

APPEARANCE: He had a large belly (symbolizing that he had the power to provide food) and breasts, and he carried lotus flowers and papyrus plants. His skin was blue or green to represent water.

JOBS/POWERS: He caused the Nile River to flood every year. When the river overflowed, the soil became dark and rich, allowing crops to grow. The river flooding was called "the arrival of Hapy."

FAMILY CONNECTIONS: Unknown.

DID YOU KNOW?

● She was born from her father's spit.

DID YOU KNOW?

● Egyptologists don't know of any temples built for him.

● Ancient Egyptians would toss lucky charms into the river for Hapy, so he would bring them a good flood.

KHEPRI — OR — KHEPER

GOD of CREATION, MOVEMENT of the SUN, and REBIRTH

PRONUNCIATION: KHEP-ree

APPEARANCE: A scarab, or a man wearing a scarab as a crown.

JOBS/POWERS: He made the sun rise each morning. The ancient Egyptians believed that Khepri, as a huge scarab, rolled the sun across the sky to the Underworld each night and brought it back up on the eastern horizon each morning to once again shine light upon the world. The sun was "reborn" each day.

FAMILY CONNECTIONS: He was self-created. Ancient Egyptians mistakenly believed that baby scarab beetles appeared out of nowhere, and they believed that Khepri was born in the same way, without parents.

BASTET

GODDESS of MUSIC and DANCE

PRONUNCIATION: BAST

APPEARANCE: A female cat; she is often shown with multiple body piercings on the ears and nose.

JOBS/POWERS: Protected Ra from harm, took care of pregnant women, protected people against contagious diseases and evil.

FAMILY CONNECTIONS: Daughter of Ra, sister of Hathor, wife of Ptah.

DID YOU KNOW?

- His name meant "to become" or "come into being."

- Charms were shaped like scarabs to bring energy to the living and reincarnation to the dead.

FUN FACT

The scarab lays its eggs in a ball of dung (yep, a ball of poop!). It rolls the perfectly round dung ball along the ground, until the baby beetles hatch and crawl out.

DID YOU KNOW?

- She killed the evil serpent god Apep.

- Egyptian women wrote the number of children they wished to have on charms and left them for her.

BES

GOD *of* CHILDBIRTH PROTECTION

PRONUNCIATION: BES

APPEARANCE: A bearded dwarf with lion features. He was ugly in order to frighten away evil spirits.

JOBS/POWERS: Watched over mothers and babies, protected against scorpion and snake bites, kept away nightmares.

FAMILY CONNECTIONS: Unknown.

TAWERET

GODDESS *of* CHILDBIRTH

PRONUNCIATION: Ta-WER-et

APPEARANCE: She had the head and body of a pregnant hippopotamus, the back of a crocodile, and the arms and legs of a lioness. All three of these animals get aggressive when their babies are threatened.

JOBS/POWERS: She fiercely protected mothers giving birth and newborn babies. Her ferocious appearance scared evil spirits away during childbirth.

FAMILY CONNECTIONS: Unknown.

DID YOU KNOW?

● There were no temples built for him. He was a household god who protected the home against demons. His picture was often found on vases and mirrors.

● Bes was one of the only gods drawn facing forward. The other gods were always pictured in profile, or sideways.

DID YOU KNOW?

● Pregnant women drank milk out of vases shaped like the goddess. "Magic wands" made out of ivory hippopotamus tusks and carved with Taweret's image were used during childbirth to keep away evil.

● The hippo and the lion used to roam Egypt but aren't found there anymore due to hunting, farming, and construction.

ALL WRITE

HIEROGLYPHS, SCRIBES, AND THE ROSETTA STONE

Can you read this?

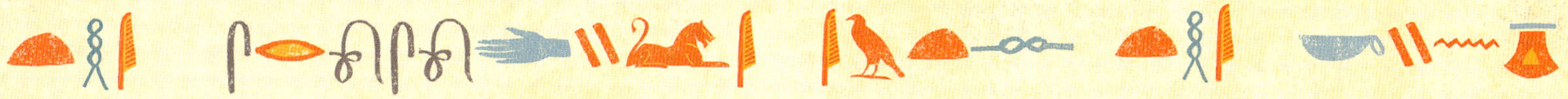

It's written in an ancient Egyptian script called hieroglyphs. Hieroglyphs means "holy writing" in Greek, and the ancient Egyptians thought the gods invented hieroglyphs.

Hieroglyphs is one of the earliest known writing systems in the world. It used small pictures instead of letters, just like a secret code. Each picture stood for a different sound, word, idea, or action. There were more than 700 different hieroglyphs! (Our alphabet has only twenty-six letters.)

Here's what the alphabet looked like:

A B C D E F G H I

J K L M N O P Q R

S T U V W X Y Z

Answer: The crocodile eats the king.

READING HIEROGLYPHS

- Only consonant letters were used: B, C, D, F, G, H, J, K, L, M, N, P, Q, R, S, T, V, W, X, Y, Z.

- The only vowel used was A. So no E, I, O, U. (They did have vowel sounds—just no symbols to show them.)

- No punctuation marks, such as commas, periods, or question marks, were used.

- There were no spaces between words.

- The English language is read from left to right in horizontal rows. Hieroglyphs can be read in any direction—in horizontal rows (from left to right or from right to left) or in vertical columns (from top to bottom). So how do you know which way to read? Look at the little pictures and find one with a head. Whichever way the head is facing is where you start reading. So if a bird's head faces right, you read from right to left.

Imagine trying to read without the help of vowels. Can you read this sentence?

**Gyptlgsts rd wrds wtht
vwls ll th tm whn thy rd hrglyphs.**

How about if both the vowels and the spaces between words are taken away? Can you read this sentence?

Thnlrvrrnsthrghgypt

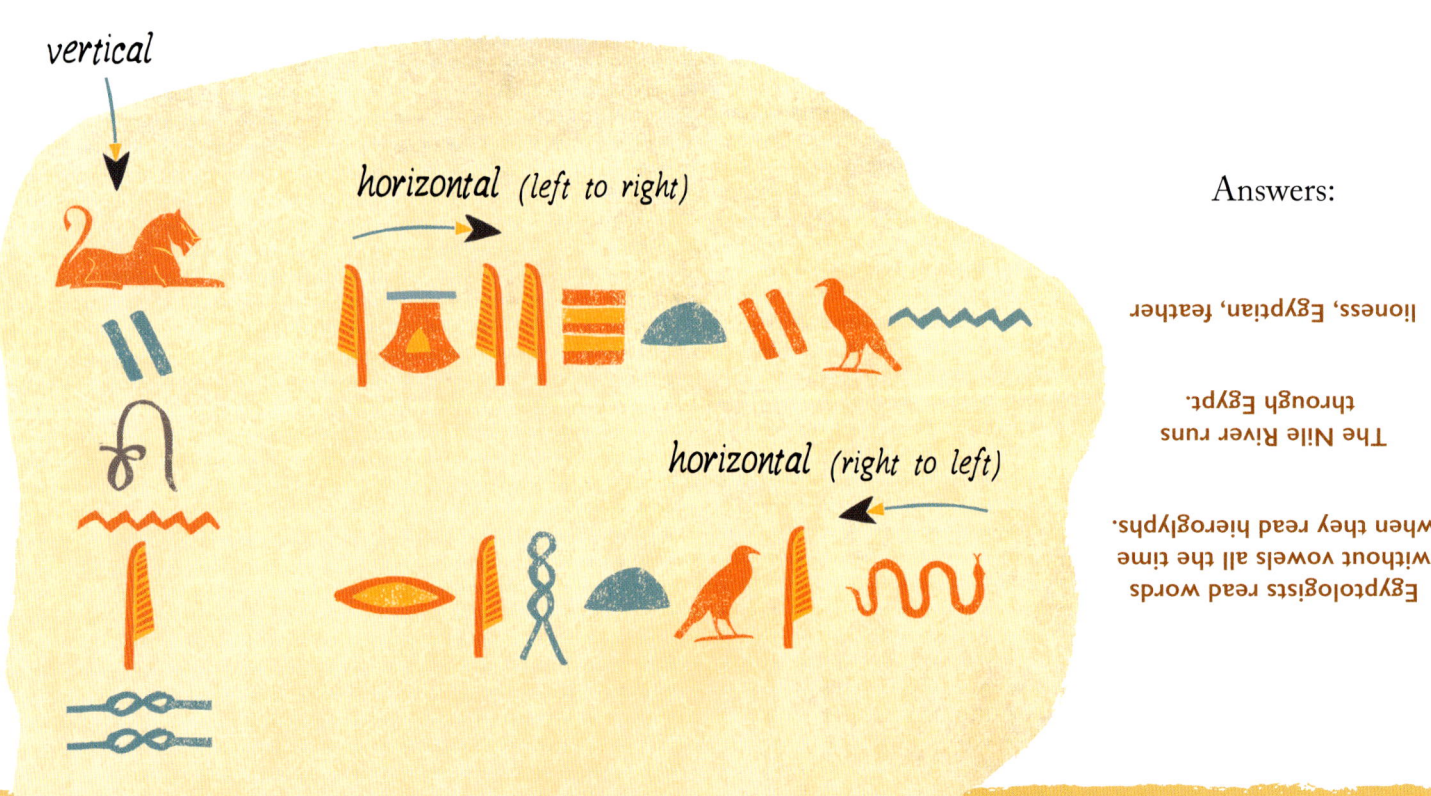

vertical

horizontal (left to right)

horizontal (right to left)

HIEROGLYPHIC NUMBERS

Numbers were also written in hieroglyphs.

- 1 is shown by one stroke.

- 10 is a drawing of the heel of a cow.

- 100 is a drawing of a coil of rope.

- 1,000 is a drawing of a lotus plant.

- 10,000 is a drawing of a finger.

- 100,000 is a drawing of a tadpole or frog.

- 1,000,000 is a drawing of a god with arms raised above his head.

A number is read by adding up the values of all the hieroglyphs.

= 99

= 9,999

What is this number?

Answer:

1,212,226

THE WRITE STUFF

Where were hieroglyphs written?

They were carved into the stone walls of temples and onto tombs where the dead were buried.

Could all ancient Egyptians write and read?

No! Back then, only about 1 in every 100 people knew how to read or write. Scribes were given the job of writing down important information. It took years of study to become a scribe. Often, if your father was a scribe, you became one, too.

How hard was it to write with hieroglyphs?

Writing hieroglyphs took a lot of time. They were only used for royal documents and for writing on temples and tomb walls. For everyday writing, scribes used much simpler kinds of hieroglyphs, called hieratic and demotic (cursive Egyptian) scripts. Some scribes wrote fictional adventure stories and letters to family and friends in hieratic script.

What was so great about scribes?

Much of what we know about ancient Egypt today comes from what the scribes wrote down all those years ago. Historians are glad the ancient Egyptians thought it was so important to keep records.

THE ROSETTA STONE

For thousands of years, no one could read hieroglyphs. Historians couldn't puzzle out what the drawings meant. Was an arm really an arm, or did it mean strength or something else? Then in 1799, French soldiers near the Egyptian village of Rosetta discovered a large, black stone tablet. The Rosetta Stone was from when Ptolemy V was king (205–180 BCE). On the stone, there were carvings in three different scripts: ancient Greek, hieroglyphs, and demotic.

In 1808, a Frenchman named Jean-François Champollion studied a copy of the stone. He could read ancient Greek and demotic and knew they said the same thing on the stone. He figured the hieroglyphs must as well. If only he could create a key to decode the symbols. . . It took him fourteen years, and in 1822, he finally figured out how to read the hieroglyphs. He realized the hieroglyphs weren't just drawings of objects—they stood for sounds and words.

Pharaohs Rule!

THE PHARAOH WAS the supreme ruler of all of ancient Egypt. He was much more than a royal or a leader of a country. He was believed to be the son of a god. Because of this, the pharaoh was made the high priest of every temple in Egypt. The pharaoh was also in charge of the government. He needed to keep the nation and the people healthy, safe, and happy.

What's the difference between the pharaoh and the king?

They're the same thing. Ancient Egyptians called their divine rulers "kings." The word "pharaoh" began to be used much later by the Greeks.

How many pharaohs were there?

There were more than 170 pharaohs during ancient Egypt's long history. (Remember, the civilization lasted for more than 3,000 years!)

Could I have been pharaoh if I'd lived back then?

Being pharaoh was a family thing, so you could only wear the crown if someone in your family had been pharaoh. The control of the country was usually kept within one family. After a pharaoh died, the crown was passed down to his eldest son, if he was able to rule. Most pharaohs were men, but there were some women pharaohs, too.

What's a dynasty?

Each time a new family group of pharaohs took the throne, it was called a dynasty. Ancient Egyptian history is divided into dynasties or time spans. Historians recognize thirty-one dynasties.

Did the pharaoh rule alone?

Family members, advisors (called viziers), and noblemen helped the pharaoh make decisions. If a pharaoh came to the throne when he was still a young boy, his mother or another female relative ruled with him. However, because the pharaoh was believed to speak directly to the gods, what he wanted to happen usually happened.

What did the vizier do?

The vizier was the highest rank in government (besides the pharaoh). He reported directly to the pharaoh, and the smaller governments throughout Egypt reported to him.

WHAT A PHARAOH WORE

URAEUS. A uraeus (an upright cobra about to strike) was perched at the top of the headdress/crown. This symbolized that the pharaoh was always ready for battle.

FAKE BEARD. Most Egyptians shaved all over, but a pharaoh sported a fake beard that was braided. Even some female pharaohs wore one!

ORNATE NECKLACE. Ancient Egyptians loved jewelry. The pharaoh often wore a thick collar necklace made from gold, precious stones, and beads.

CROOK. The pharaoh held a crook, a cane with a hooked handle that shepherds used to gather their sheep. This symbolized that the pharaoh cared for his people.

A KILT. A pleated kilt was worn around the waist for ceremonies. But, since Egypt gets quite cold in the winter, the pharaoh would have dressed in something warmer then.

NEMES HEADDRESS. The nemes was a striped cloth that tied at the back of the head. It looked like a lion's mane and symbolized the pharaoh's power.

MAKEUP. Both males and females wore kohl around their eyes, rouge, and perfumed oils. The makeup may have helped protect their eyes and faces from the sun, flies, and infections.

FLAIL. The pharaoh held a flail, a rod with three strands of beads attached to the top, which was either a weapon used by shepherds to defend their flock or a tool to thresh grain. This symbolized that the pharaoh was a protector and a provider of food.

How much money did a pharaoh have?

None! Money hadn't been invented yet—Egypt was a cashless society. But, even so, the pharaoh was massively wealthy. The pharaoh lived in an enormous palace decked out with jewels and gold and packed with fancy stuff. He had hundreds of servants.

How many wives did a pharaoh have?

Most pharaohs had one main wife, and she was the queen, but they often had other wives as well. Oftentimes they married their own family members to be sure outsiders couldn't inherit the throne.

Famous Pharaohs

KHUFU

ALSO KNOWN AS: Cheops (his name in Greek).

LENGTH OF RULE: About twenty-six or so years; probably became pharaoh in his twenties.

CLAIM TO FAME

- He built the Great Pyramid of Giza—the largest pyramid in Egypt. It took his workers between ten and twenty years to build it.

- His life is a mystery. Little is known about it.

DEATH DETAILS

🔴 The only complete statue of him ever found is tiny—just three inches high (7.5 centimeters), about the size of a crayon—which is funny, since his pyramid was so enormous!

🔴 Two large ships were discovered in graves beside his pyramid. They were probably meant for him to use in the afterlife.

🔴 His mummy was never found. Neither was any of his treasure.

RAMSES II

ALSO KNOWN AS: Ramses the Great, the great builder.

LENGTH OF RULE: At least sixty-five years, which is thought to be the second-longest time for any pharaoh. He became pharaoh at age twenty-five.

CLAIM TO FAME

- He was a mighty warrior. He led the Egyptian army to victory in many battles and expanded the Egyptian empire. From this, he brought great wealth to Egypt.

- He left his mark. He constructed more monuments and had more statues built of himself than any other pharaoh. He carved his name all over Egypt—even on statues of other pharaohs—and even had their statues destroyed so he could use the building material to create statues of himself!

- He put peace in writing. He signed the first recorded peace treaty. It was with the Hittites, an ancient people.

- He had more than 100 kids!

DEATH DETAILS

● He was buried in the Valley of Kings.

● His mummy is now in the Egyptian Museum in Cairo, Egypt.

● After he died, nine other pharaohs took the name Ramses in his honor.

AKHENATEN

ALSO KNOWN AS: Amenhotep IV.

LENGTH OF RULE: Sixteen years. He wasn't supposed to be crowned pharaoh but his older brother died, so he was next in line.

CLAIM TO FAME

- He changed ancient Egyptian religion. He declared the god Aten (also a sun god like Ra) the only god of Egypt and outlawed all other gods. This was a bold move—no pharaoh had ever messed around with the tradition of worshipping many gods. People were not happy.

- He got rid of all the priests. He said he was the only link to Aten.

- He introduced a new, realistic style of art. Before this, artists only drew people with stiff, "perfect" bodies. Now they began to draw people that looked more natural, and put them in everyday settings, such as playing with children.

- He ruled when life was good. Ancient Egypt's wealthiest period occurred during his reign.

- His queen was the famous Nefertiti. King Tut was his son.

DEATH DETAILS

- After his death, ancient Egyptians went back to worshipping many gods. His one-god idea hadn't been very popular.

- Ancient Egyptians erased his name from their histories—and even took it off their official list of pharaohs.

TUTANKHAMUN

ALSO KNOWN AS: King Tut, the Boy King, Tutankhaten.

LENGTH OF RULE: About nine years. He was about nine years old when he took power. He died around age eighteen.

CLAIM TO FAME

- He brought back the old religious system. He rejected the only-one-god rule and allowed Egyptians to worship many gods. He even changed his name from Tutankhaten to Tutankhamun to show he was different from Akhenaten, who believed in only one god.

- He needed help running the country. Because he was so young, his vizier and army general ruled for him. His vizier took over after he died.

- He ruled when life was still good. During his reign, Egypt was the most powerful country in the world.

DEATH DETAILS

● He became famous not for what he did while alive but because—thousands of years after his death—his tomb was discovered, filled with treasure.

● Egyptologists don't know for sure how he died.

FAMOUS FEMALE PHARAOHS

ANCIENT EGYPT DID have female rulers. There weren't many compared with all the male rulers, but they had many more than most other ancient civilizations (and some modern ones, too).

men allowed a woman from the royal family to rule until a suitable male was found or grew up. But a few times, these female pharaohs claimed the throne fully for themselves.

If *king* and *pharaoh* were different names for the same thing, did it work like that for *queen* and *pharaoh*?

No. *Queen* was the title given to the chief wife of the king. Throughout history there have been many queens, but only a few female pharaohs.

Were women and men treated equally in ancient Egypt?

Unlike elsewhere in the world, women in ancient Egypt had high status. They were able to own and inherit property, run a business, divorce, and remarry. But even though they had equal legal rights, they weren't treated as equals. Women could not go to school and were expected to take care of the home and the family.

How did a woman become pharaoh?

By custom, men were supposed to be crowned pharaoh. Often women were given the title of "regent," and this allowed them to rule alongside their husbands, brothers, or sons. If the pharaoh was a young boy (becoming pharaoh because his father had just died), his mother would step in until the boy was old enough to take over. Ancient Egyptians believed pharaohs should come from within the same family. In order to stop an "outsider" from seizing the throne, the

Why were some brothers and sisters made to marry?

To keep the power in the royal family. It was feared that if a pharaoh married an "outsider," that new person's parents, brothers, or cousins would try to take control of the throne.

THE POWER THREE

Hatshepsut, Nefertiti, and Cleopatra were three of the best-known female rulers.

HATSHEPSUT

HOW SHE CAME TO RULE

HATSHEPSUT WAS THE daughter of pharaoh Thutmose I. When her father died, her husband (and half brother) Thutmose II was crowned pharaoh and she was made queen. Then her husband died. The next male in line was her nephew, Thutmose III, but he was just a young child. Hatshepsut was made regent to help her nephew rule. But Hatshepsut wanted more respect, since she was the one doing the hard work and the ruling anyway. So she had herself made co-ruler. She reigned for the next twenty years. This was the longest reign of a female pharaoh.

CLAIM TO FAME

• She encouraged trade with other lands. It was a time of peace and great wealth. She left the country in better shape than it had been when she took power.

• She built many monuments and statues, and hundreds of buildings. She promoted art and architecture.

IN DEATH

• Thutmose III took power after Hatshepsut died, and he tried to wipe away all evidence that she had ruled. He had his aunt's name chiseled off buildings and destroyed many of her statues and monuments.

• Her mummy was discovered in the Valley of the Kings. From her mummy, scientists learned that when she died she was only five feet tall, obese, and suffered from bone cancer and diabetes.

NEFERTITI
HOW SHE CAME TO RULE

NEFERTITI BECAME QUEEN when she married Pharaoh Akhenaten. In ancient Egypt, marriages were often a business arrangement between families. But, based on his writings and artworks showing them together and as a family, Nefertiti and Akhenaten seemed to be truly in love. Her husband treated her as an equal, and they ruled together as a power couple. It's believed that she only gave birth to daughters. After Akhenaten died, Tutankhamun (whose father was Akhenaten but had a different mother; however, he married one of Nefertiti's daughters) took the throne.

FUN FACT

A sculpture of her head is one of the most recognized pieces of ancient Egyptian art.

CLAIM TO FAME

Nefertiti and her husband changed the country's religion, only allowing the worship of a single god—the sun god.

IN DEATH

• No one knows exactly when she died.

• Her tomb has not yet been discovered.

FUN FACT

Her name means "a beautiful woman has come."

CLEOPATRA
HOW SHE CAME TO RULE

CLEOPATRA WAS BORN in Egypt, but her family was Greek. They had been ruling Egypt for 300 years, and her father was the pharaoh. When her father died, eighteen-year-old Cleopatra and her ten-year-old brother Ptolemy XIII were made co-pharaohs. In keeping with tradition, they were married. Cleopatra took control, and she was a great ruler. But as her brother grew older, he wanted more power. He had his sister banished to Syria, a nearby country, so he could rule by himself.

Cleopatra refused to be pushed out. She returned to Egypt, hiring her own army and paying them in gold. She'd heard the Roman general Julius Caesar was visiting the palace. Cleopatra figured that if she could team up with Caesar, together they could defeat her brother. But there was a problem. Her brother had instructed the guards not to let her into the palace. How would she talk with Caesar? Then she had a sneaky idea.

She dressed in her finest clothes and best jewelry and had her servant wrap her in what many

Egyptologists believe was a linen sack used for holding sheets. He carried the sack past the guards and into Caesar's rooms in the palace. He presented it as a gift, opening it onto the floor. And out tumbled beautiful Cleopatra! Caesar was stunned—and, of course, fell in love. Cleopatra asked him to help her—and he did. Caesar's army defeated her brother's army, and it's believed her brother drowned in the Nile River while trying to escape.

Her family had her marry her other younger brother, thirteen-year-old Ptolemy XIV, so they could rule together. Cleopatra and Caesar went to Rome, and they had a baby named Caesarion. Then Caesar was killed by Roman senators. Fearing for her safety, Cleopatra returned to Egypt. She had her brother poisoned and her sister sent away, so they could never block her son from becoming pharaoh. (This type of cruelty was common in

FUN FACT

Ancient Egyptians— and Cleopatra herself— thought she was the living goddess Isis.

43

the royal families.) Then she co-ruled Egypt with her baby son (but, really, all by herself).

The Egyptian people loved her, and the country did well. But Cleopatra was concerned that Octavian (also known as Augustus), who'd taken over as ruler in Rome after Caesar, would invade Egypt. She didn't want Egypt governed by another country. She needed help. Dressed as the goddess Isis, she sailed on a golden boat with purple sails to meet a Roman general named Marc Antony. He, too, was dazzled by her and fell in love. They married and had three children. They combined armies and fought Octavian's army in a big battle at sea but lost terribly.

Cleopatra and Marc Antony returned to Egypt. Then Octavian's army came after them. Marc Antony went back to the battlefield but soon realized he was about to be captured by Octavian. And then he heard the horrible news—Cleopatra had died! He killed himself with his own sword. But the rumor wasn't true. Cleopatra was alive! Octavian had taken her prisoner and threatened to parade her through the streets. Fearing this humiliation and sad about Marc Antony's death, Cleopatra had a cobra smuggled in to her in a basket of fruit. According to the stories, she used the snake's poisonous venom to kill herself. She was thirty-nine years old.

FUN FACT

According to legends, she took baths in donkey milk to keep her skin soft!

WHY DOES CLEOPATRA'S LIFE SOUND MORE INTERESTING THAN THE LIVES OF THE OTHER FEMALE RULERS?

Unlike the others, Cleopatra's life has always been told like a story. Cleopatra's writings never survived, and there aren't any firsthand accounts (written by someone who knew her) of her life. Many years later, the Greek historian Plutarch and the playwright William Shakespeare (both born after she died) helped to shape her story and make it so popular.

CLAIM TO FAME

• She was in power for twenty-one years.

• She was very smart. She spoke nine languages and wrote many scientific and political books. Unlike her family, who only spoke Greek, she learned Egyptian so she could speak to the people she ruled.

• She made the Egyptian empire larger and wealthier by trading with many different nations.

IN DEATH

She was believed to be buried with Marc Antony. Her burial place and mummy have yet to be found.

THE JOURNEY TO THE AFTERLIFE

ALL ANCIENT EGYPTIANS believed that life went on after they died, and they called this "the afterlife."

What did they think the afterlife would be like?

Just like life in Egypt—only *much* better. They'd get to relax in a heavenly place, where there would be parties and plenty of food to eat. And the pharaoh had the added bonus of coming back as a god. He'd ride with the sun god Ra across the sky, making sure life was good for everyone in Egypt.

Why did the ancient Egyptians think about death so much?

Back then, not many people lived past the age of forty, and life in the desert was hard. Life on earth was part of the journey to the afterlife.

Did all dead people make it to the afterlife?

The journey to the afterlife was tricky—and not everyone made it.

CHECKLIST FOR GETTING TO THE AFTERLIFE

☑ Make sure the dead body is preserved to keep the soul alive forever. (Mummification is the way to do this.)

☑ Pack everything that person will need in the afterlife. Place it—along with the mummified body—in a sealed tomb.

☑ Be sure people continue to speak the name of the dead.

☑ Have family members bring fresh bread and beer to the tomb.

☑ Send the soul to travel through the Underworld, also called Duat. The god Anubis will lead the way. Don't forget to bring the Book of the Dead.

☑ If the soul makes it through, the dead person will be judged on how honorably they lived their life. They'll only be allowed into the afterlife if judged to be a good person. If not, they will be eaten by the evil god Ammit.

BOOK OF THE DEAD

The Book of the Dead is a collection of nearly 200 magic spells. The dead used it like a road map to help guide them through the obstacle course of the Underworld. It held the answers to the tricky questions gods asked, clues on which way to go, and spells to say to get safely past the dangers. The Book of the Dead was written on rolls of papyrus and placed in each tomb. Parts of it have also been discovered carved or painted on walls of tombs and coffins.

LAKE of FIRE

THE TWELVE GATES

The dead didn't automatically get into the after-life. Everyone had to battle their way through the Underworld. The Underworld was a magical land filled with dangers. There was a lake of fire, walls of iron, poisonous snakes, ferocious crocodiles, terrifying beasts, and many traps. The dead had to make it through twelve different gates. Each gate had a guardian. To enter, the dead had to answer tricky questions or perform scary deeds.

HALL of
FINAL
JUDGEMENT

HALL of
MA'AT

THE JUDGING

If the dead made it all the way through the Underworld, they'd reach the Hall of Final Judgment. Here, they stood in front of the god Osiris and forty-two divine judges. First they had to correctly name all forty-two judges. (That's *a lot* of names to remember!) Then they were questioned about everything they were suspected of having done wrong in life. The Book of the Dead gave instructions on what to say. Spell 125, the longest in the book, was a "Negative Confession" to recite. It listed forty-two crimes the dead had to have not done, such as:

> "I have not killed."
> "I have not robbed."
> "I have not lied."
> "I have not eavesdropped."
> "I have not spoken in anger."
> "I have not shut my ears to the truth."

Next stop was the Hall of Ma'at, also called the Hall of Two Truths. To make it to the afterlife, the dead needed to be ferried on the god Ra's boat. But to be allowed on the boat, their heart had to be light. So the god Anubis weighed the heart on a scale against the Feather of Truth, which belonged to the goddess Ma'at. Then the god Thoth recorded the weight. If the heart was light (meaning the person had done good deeds in life), they were ferried to the afterlife. If it was heavy, the evil god Ammit appeared—and gobbled them up!

ALL ABOUT MUMMIES

What is a mummy?

A mummy is a dead body that's been dried out so it will last a long, long, long time.

What happens to a dead body if you don't dry it out?

It decomposes, or rots. Bacteria grow in wet places, and a human body is about 60 percent water. When people die, bacteria make flesh and organs rot. That's why, after several days, a dead body will smell bad and turn green and black. Think of it like this: Which will rot faster if you leave it out on the kitchen counter—a juicy steak or a stick of beef jerky? The steak, because jerky is dried out—just like a mummy.

Who made the first mummy in ancient Egypt?

The first mummies were made by accident. The land along the Nile River was being used for farming, so dead bodies were buried in the desert. The hot, dry sand sucked all the moisture out of the bodies and naturally mummified them.

Did only the Egyptians make mummies?

No, but they did have the most famous ones! The people of South America were wrapping mummies 2,000 years before the Egyptians. Mummies have been discovered in countries all over the world, including in China, Peru, and Mexico.

How long did it take to make a mummy?

About seventy days.

Did everyone in ancient Egypt get turned into a mummy?

All royalty, their families, and high-ranking officials got the full-on, first-class mummy treatment. Many regular-folk Egyptians were mummified, too, but they were given the budget plan, because mummification was expensive. That meant no fancy masks, no gold, and no fresh cloth bandages. A lot of Egyptians weren't mummified but instead were buried in pits in the desert.

Why did they mummify bodies?

Ancient Egyptians thought that a person was made up of his or her physical body and his or her soul. The soul was the spirit, personality, and energy. They believed the body and the soul separated when a person died. But the soul and the body (in good condition!) needed to reconnect to enter the afterlife. If the body was destroyed, the soul would be lost. Mummification let a human body "live forever" and allowed the soul to recognize the body it belonged with.

What's the story with the soul?

Ancient Egyptians believed a person's soul had several parts.

The **KA** was the life force—kind of like a "double" of the person. Breathing, eating, and drinking helped keep it strong. The ka left the body after death, but stayed in the tomb, using all the objects buried there.

The **BA** was the personality, the thing that made each person unique. It would fly out of the tomb and into the world to watch over the dead person's family during the day and return at night to rest. It was drawn as a human-headed bird.

The **AKH**, or the spirit, was formed when the ka and ba came together after death. The akh had to travel through the Underworld to reach the afterlife, while the ka and the ba stayed behind in the tomb with the mummified body. It was believed only "good" people had an akh. Once the akh made it to the afterlife, it needed its body to live again.

A person's **SHADOW** was believed to be attached to their feet in life. In death, it got a life of its own.

A person's **NAME** was their identity. If a dead person's name was not written down somewhere, the ka and the ba wouldn't be able to find the body and would wander around lost forever.

A STEP-BY-STEP GUIDE TO MAKING A MUMMY

Bring the dead body to the **EMBALMER PRIESTS**.

Wash the dead body in **NILE RIVER WATER** and palm wine.

Call in a priest to make a slit in the left side of the body and remove the liver, lungs, stomach, and intestines. (Sometimes the heart was kept in the body.) Save the organs in **CANOPIC JARS**. Pull out the brain and throw the brain away. (This happened in some mummies but not all.)

Pack the body with **NATRON**, a drying salt, which soaks up all the body's liquids so the body won't rot. Wait forty days before removing the salts.

The body is now shriveled like a raisin, so it needs to be stuffed with cloth, sand, and sawdust to give it back its shape. Perfume it with **MYRRH** and soften the leathery skin with oils.

Add some **FAKE EYES**. Little onions were often used, or glass beads or stones.

EMBALMER PRIESTS

NILE RIVER WATER

OPENING OF THE MOUTH CEREMONY

FAKE EYES

NATRON

MYRHH

Now it's wrapping time. Wrap the body with long strips of **LINEN CLOTH**. Tuck precious jewels and lucky charms called **AMULETS** into the cloth.

Slather the cloth with warm **RESIN**. The resin will harden and keep out bacteria.

Perform the **OPENING OF THE MOUTH CEREMONY**.

Cover face with a **MUMMY MASK**.

Wrap the body with more strips of linen cloth.

Place the mummy inside a wooden **MUMMY CASE** or coffin to protect it from robbers and animals. Paint sides of the case with symbols and blessings. Seal it up.

LINEN CLOTH

MUMMY CASE

AMULETS

MUMMY MASK

CANOPIC JARS

RESIN

EMBALMER PRIESTS—These priests knew anatomy, or how the body is put together. They were in charge of making mummies. They wore jackal masks in honor of Anubis, the god of mummification.

CANOPIC JARS—The internal organs were stored in four jars. Each jar had a lid shaped like the head of the god who protected that organ. The four gods were the sons of the god Horus. The jars were stored in a box called the canopic chest and placed near the mummy inside the tomb.

IMSETY

QEBEHSENUEF

DUAMUTEF

HAPY

- The liver was protected by **IMSETY**, who had a human head.
- The intestines were protected by **QEBEHSENUEF**, who had a falcon head.
- The stomach was protected by **DUAMUTEF**, who had a jackal head.
- The lungs were protected by **HAPY** (not to be confused with the god of flooding, also named Hapy), who had a baboon head.

HEART—To the ancient Egyptians, the heart was the most important organ. They believed it was the center of intelligence and that people thought with their hearts.

BRAIN—Egyptians tossed away the brain, because they thought it was useless. To get the brain out of the body, a metal hook was inserted through the nostril and the brain was mashed up and jiggled back out through the nose.

NATRON—A drying salt that soaks up the body's liquids, so the body won't rot. Salt is a desiccant, meaning it removes water. Have you ever eaten salty chips and then felt very thirsty? That's because the salt pulled water out of the cells in your body. The same thing happens if you sprinkle fresh vegetables with salt—they shrivel because the water is taken out. Mummification works the same way—the salts dry out the dead body.

MYRRH—A scented oil that comes from tree sap. The sap is hardened and heated to make the sweet-smelling oil.

LINEN CLOTH—Ancient Egyptians saved linen throughout their lives so they'd have enough ready to wrap their dead body. It often took fifteen days to fully wrap a mummy. One mummy discovered had twenty layers of bandages!

MUMMIES TELL ALL

Scientists spend years studying, scanning, and x-raying mummies. They've been able to learn:

- The age of the person at death

- The sex of the person

- Hair color (King Ramses II had red hair!)

- The cause of death

- What the person used to eat

- Diseases or injuries he or she had

- If the person was royalty or not

AMULETS—Amulets were small charms thought to have magical powers to protect the mummy and bring good luck in the next life.

RESIN—The sticky sap from trees that was used to glue the linen strips together.

MUMMY MASK—A mask was placed over the mummy's head. A pharaoh's royal mask was made out of gold and decorated with jewels. Masks for non-royals were made out of cartonnage, a kind of papier-mâché. All masks were painted with portraits of the dead (they were painted as young and good-looking, no matter what their age when they died), so the soul could find the right body in the afterlife.

MUMMY CASE—Early mummy cases were rectangular, but later on they were human-shaped. If the dead person was wealthy, his mummy was placed inside two or three cases for extra protection. The outermost wooden case was painted with a picture of the dead person. (Sometimes coffins were made in advance and painted with random faces.)

SYMBOLS—The sides of the coffin were painted with pictures of the gods, blessings, and spells to help guide the dead on their journey to the afterlife. Some symbols painted on mummy cases were:

- A scarab beetle—the symbol of rebirth.
- A winged sun/falcon—the symbol of the god Horus, for protection.
- An eye—the symbol of healing.
- An ankh—the Egyptian symbol of life.

Mummify an Apple!

WHAT YOU NEED

- A small apple
- A vegetable peeler
- A Popsicle stick or a pumpkin-carving tool (only use tool with help from an adult)
- ½ cup salt—table salt, sea salt, or kosher salt
- ½ cup baking soda
- Zip-close plastic bag

WHAT YOU DO

1. Peel the skin off the apple with the vegetable peeler.
2. Using the Popsicle stick or the pumpkin-carving tool, carve a face in the apple.
3. Place the apple in the plastic bag.
4. Combine an equal amount of salt and baking soda to fully coat the apple in the bag.
5. Leave the bag open and upright (you want the moisture to escape). Leave your apple in the bag for one to two weeks. Keep it away from direct sunlight.
6. Take out the apple and see how the salt mixture has mummified it.

Do not eat the apple or the mummifying ingredients!

WEIRD BUT TRUE MUMMY FACTS

- Ramses II's mummy had peppercorns stuffed up his nose to give it shape.

- Fingers and toes were often individually wrapped. If one broke off, a priest would replace it with a piece of wood.

- Some mummies had their fingernails painted with henna, an orange dye.

- If the intestines were lost or cut by mistake during removal, a piece of rope was put in the jar instead.

- In 1976 (3,000 years after he died!), King Ramses II's (also spelled Ramesses) mummy had to get an Egyptian passport. The rule is that any person—living or dead—leaving the country needs an official passport, and the mummy was being flown to France for scientists' help preserving it. On the passport, his job was listed as "King (deceased)."

- Yuya, the great-grandfather of King Tutunkhamun, is the best-preserved Egyptian mummy. When he was unwrapped, he still had his eyelashes, eyebrows, beard stubble, blond hair, and fingernails!

- Royal mummies were usually positioned with their arms crossed over their bodies.

FULL NAME
RAMESSES II

DATE OF BIRTH
--/--/1303BC

NATIONALITY
EGYPTIAN

PROFESSION: KING (DECEASED)

P < RAMESSES <<II <<<<<<<<<<<< <<<<<<
A17734243EGY68144M<<<<<<<<<<<<02

ANIMAL MUMMIES

HUMANS WEREN'T THE only ones mummified in death—animals were, too!

Animals were extremely important to the ancient Egyptians. They were seen as the living forms of gods. This is why their gods had animal-shaped heads and bodies. Killing an animal associated with a god was a serious crime—sometimes punishable by death!

Animals were mummified as gifts to the gods in exchange for good fortune. Falcons were mummified for Horus, cats for Bastet, dogs for Anubis, and ibises and baboons for Thoth. Stalls selling mummified animals were set up outside temples. People would buy one to leave as an offering to a god. X-rays have shown that some of these mummy gifts-to-the-gods didn't contain actual bodies but were fakes wrapped up to fool the long lines of eager buyers.

However, it's believed that more than 70 million real animals were mummified—dogs, cats, foxes, baboons, monkeys, crocodiles, horses, lions, goats, rams, shrews, and even frogs. Like humans, they were carefully dried out, wrapped, and placed in coffins. Animal cemeteries, each one dedicated to a certain type of animal, have been found throughout the land. One had more than 400 baboons buried in it!

FUN FACT

Egyptians made "meat mummies," dried parts of an animal, such as duck wings or legs of beef, to eat for food in the afterlife.

The ancient Egyptians mummified their beloved pets, too. Pets were buried in the tomb with them or right outside, so they could all be together again in the afterlife.

CATS

- Cats were the favorite animal and honored household pets. They were considered magical and often sacrificed to the goddess Bastet to bring good luck.

- Cats were used to keep snakes and rodents away from food. Sometimes people brought them out hunting, too.

- The Egyptian name for "cat" was "miw," which is the sound that the cats make. The ancient Egyptians didn't give their cats names, but they did like to dress them up in jewelry.

- When a family cat died, all family members shaved their eyebrows to show their grief. They were expected to mourn the cat until their eyebrows grew fully back.

- Thousands of cats were mummified, and many were buried in cat-shaped coffins. Often mummified rats and mice were buried with them to chase and eat in the afterlife.

- Ancient Egyptians were in awe of the big cats—lions, leopards, cheetahs—and kings were called "as fearless as a lion." Some royals tamed cheetahs and kept them as pets. King Ramses II had a lion as a pet! He named him Slayer of His Enemies.

- Popular breeds were basenjis, greyhounds, salukis, pharaoh hounds, and mastiffs.

- One human mummy was discovered buried with his mummified dog curled up at his feet.

MONKEYS

- Monkeys and baboons were household pets. Art from that time shows monkeys on leashes.

BULLS

- The Apis bull was a sacred bull worshipped by ancient Egyptians.

DOGS

- Dogs were also "man's best friend" in ancient Egypt, and unlike cats, these household pets were given names. They were used for hunting and guarding.

- Many dogs wore fancy leather collars.

FUN FACT

Ancient Egyptians didn't ride camels. They weren't introduced to Egypt and tamed to ride until after the ancient Egyptian civilization ended.

CROCODILES

- Many crocodile mummies have been discovered. One even had forty-seven small mummified crocodiles hidden inside it!

- Crocodiles were feared, because they were so ferocious. People hoped that if they prayed to the crocodile god, Sobek, he'd stay happy and not let crocodiles attack them. Crocodiles were often hunted to be killed, mummified, and presented as gifts to Sobek.

- Ancient Egyptians tried to keep crocodiles as pets. They even dressed them up in jewelry. But it didn't take long to realize that these dangerous animals didn't make good snuggle buddies!

- There was a city in ancient Egypt that the Greeks called "Crocodile City," because everyone there worshipped Sobek. A sacred crocodile was kept in a special temple pond. The crocodile was decorated with precious gems and gold. Priests took care of it day and night. Visitors brought gifts of food, and the priests' job was to pry open the crocodile's mouth and feed it. When the crocodile died, it was given an elaborate funeral and mummified with linen bandages. Then another crocodile was chosen to take its place.

SERVANTS

MUU
DANCERS

FAMILY
MEMBERS

WOMEN
MOURNERS

SLED

THE BURIAL

ONCE THE MUMMIFICATION was finished, it was time for the burial. Family, friends, servants, and priests walked behind the coffin in a funeral procession to the burial site. It was like a big parade. Every person carried something the dead would need in the afterlife—food, games, chests of clothes, furniture, jewelry. It was believed that the more people who showed up to cry and say goodbye, the better the dead person's chance of entering the afterlife. A huge crowd meant the dead had been loved and respected in life.

Sometimes WOMEN MOURNERS were hired to cry at funerals. Even if they hadn't known the dead, it was their job to sob and wail loudly, as if their hearts were breaking.

The coffin was dragged on a SLED. A smaller sled was used to pull the chest of canopic jars.

FAMILY MEMBERS showed they were in mourning; the men did not shave, and women tore their clothing and rubbed dust on their heads.

PRIESTS chanted prayers and spells and burned incense.

SERVANTS brought oils, food, and other items for the funeral.

MUU DANCERS, wearing reed crowns and kilts, performed at the entrance to the tomb.

PRIESTS

59

OPEN WIDE!

When the funeral procession reached the burial site, a priest performed rituals on the mummified body. The most important was the Opening of the Mouth ceremony. The priest touched the eyes and the mouth with a special instrument to "open" them. Now the body would be able to see, eat, and speak in the afterlife.

SEALED TIGHT

The mummified body was sealed in its coffin, then placed in a sarcophagus, or a stone coffin. The sarcophagus kept the mummy safe from animals and tomb robbers. Later sarcophagi were shaped and painted to look like the pharaoh.

CARTOUCHES

If the dead king's name was forgotten or not written down anywhere, it was believed the ba and ka would get lost, and the king would disappear forever without reaching the afterlife. So a cartouche was attached to the royal coffin and sarcophagus. A cartouche was like a name tag. It was oval shaped, and the dead's name was written in hieroglyphs inside it.

A horizontal line was drawn at the end. The oval surrounding the cartouche acted like a fence, protecting the name (and the king) from evil spirits in life and in death.

SEE YOU SOON

Once the sarcophagus was sealed, the family had a big feast by the entrance to the tomb. But it wasn't a goodbye party. They believed they'd see each other in the afterlife, and the dead's ba would visit the living in the form of a bird and return to the tomb on feast days to have meals with their family.

PYRAMIDS

THE EARLY PHARAOHS built pyramids as royal burial spots. Deep inside these triangular-shaped tombs, the mummified pharaohs and everything they needed in the afterlife were sealed up in special rooms. So far, more than 138 pyramids have been discovered in the Egyptian desert.

How old are the pyramids?

Super old! They date back to the beginning of ancient Egyptian history—over 4,000 years ago.

Before the pyramids, where were mummies buried?

Early mummies were buried in pit graves and then under rectangular tombs called mastabas. A mastaba had a flat roof and slanted sides, and looked like a large stone bench. Mummies were placed in a special chamber underneath the mastaba.

Who built the first pyramid?

King Djoser wanted to be buried in the most beautiful tomb ever, so he instructed Imhotep, his architect, to design something much fancier than a mastaba. Imhotep stacked six mastabas, one on top of the other. Each mastaba was smaller than the one below it. His design is called a step pyramid—and Egyptologists believe it was designed to look like a stairway up to the heavens.

Wait—wasn't Imhotep one of the Egyptian gods?

He was! After he died, he was worshipped as the god of medicine. In addition to being an architect, Imhotep was a famous healer.

STEP PYRAMID

Who made the first smooth-sided pyramid?

King Snefru did. He instructed his architects to build a pyramid without any steps. The Bent Pyramid was an experiment with this new design. The angle of its sides changed during construction, so it came out a bit lopsided or bent. No mummies were buried there. King Snefru's architect tried again, and the Red Pyramid (named after the red limestone stones used to build its core) was much closer to a true pyramid shape. King Snefru's son Khufu, who became pharaoh after him, perfected this design and created the Great Pyramid of Giza. Egyptologists believe the smooth sides symbolized the rays of the sun and connected the pharaoh to the sun god Ra.

BENT PYRAMID

Who did the work of building the pyramids?

Thousands of peasant workers. They were *not* slaves. The workers were given meals of bread and beer, as well as clothing and a place to live in a nearby village.

How big are the pyramids?

The pyramids are our original skyscrapers. A few are big enough to be seen from outer space!

Why were all pyramids built on the west side of the Nile River?

The sun rises in the east, so the river's east side was considered the side of birth. The west side was associated with death, because that's where the sun set—or "died"—each night.

SMOOTH PYRAMID

A STEP-BY-STEP GUIDE TO BUILDING A PYRAMID

IT'S ALWAYS BEEN a mystery how the pyramids were built, since the technology we rely on today did not exist back then. While some pyramids took a few years to build, others took about twenty years.

Here's how many Egyptologists think it was done:

- **Planning.** Pharaohs started designing and building their pyramids as soon as they became king. An architect along with scribes planned out every detail. They did math equations to calculate the pyramid's exact angles and the number of bricks needed. Rope was used to measure distances.

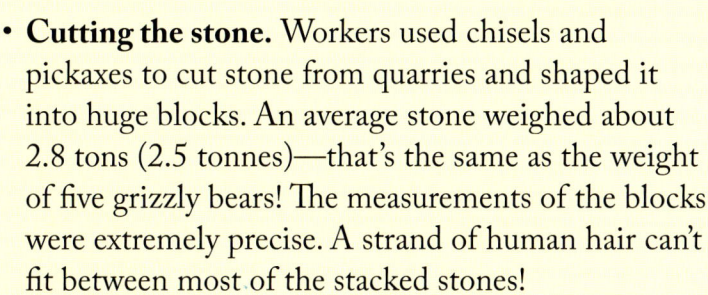

- **Moving the stone.** The wheel hadn't been invented yet, so there were no trucks, no carts, and no wheelbarrows. So how were all those heavy blocks moved from the quarry to the building site? On a large sled! Have you ever dragged something heavy through the sand? It's not easy. What you're dragging sinks into the sand, as sand piles up in front of it. Egyptologists think workers solved this problem by wetting the sand to make it harder and more compact—the same way you wet sand to build a sturdy sand castle.

- **Cutting the stone.** Workers used chisels and pickaxes to cut stone from quarries and shaped it into huge blocks. An average stone weighed about 2.8 tons (2.5 tonnes)—that's the same as the weight of five grizzly bears! The measurements of the blocks were extremely precise. A strand of human hair can't fit between most of the stacked stones!

- **Lifting the stone.** How did the workers lift these heavy stones into place? The stones were placed on wooden sleds. They were pulled—by the workers or teams of oxen—up a system of ramps made out of mud and gravel. Some ramps were a mile long! The ramps were taken down after the pyramid was built.

PARTS OF A PYRAMID

At the top was the **CAPSTONE**. It was made of granite and covered in a mixture of gold and silver.

The **OUTER BLOCKS** were smooth. They were made from white limestone and shone bright in the desert sun.

The **INNER BLOCKS** were rough. They were made from local limestone.

The **ENTRANCE** was often hidden to stop robbers.

The **FOUR SIDES** faced north, south, east, and west. They were lined up using the stars.

The **BASE** of a pyramid was always a perfect square. (Except for the very first pyramid—Djoser's step pyramid has a rectangular base.)

Build Your Own Pyramid

WHAT YOU NEED

- A large box of sugar cubes
- A piece of sturdy cardboard, cut into an 8-inch by 8-inch square (or whatever size you want your pyramid to be)
- White tacky glue (thin glue will melt the sugar) or cake icing
- Paint (sandy brown color), craft sand, or gold glitter spray
- Paintbrush

WHAT YOU DO

1. Arrange 64 sugar cubes in 8 rows of 8 cubes on the cardboard square to form the base of your pyramid. Glue down each cube individually or first paint the cardboard with a layer of glue or icing and then arrange them.

2. Add the second layer to the pyramid. Using 49 cubes, glue them down in 7 rows of 7 cubes on the center of the first layer.

> **Don't have sugar cubes? Try building a step pyramid out of Lego bricks!**

3. Glue down the other layers. Each layer should be 1 cube smaller than the previous layer, so 6 by 6 (36 cubes), 5 by 5 (25 cubes), 4 by 4 (16 cubes), 3 by 3 (9 cubes), 2 by 2 (4 cubes), and finally a single sugar cube on top.

4. Let the glue dry for several hours.

5. Gently paint the pyramid a sandy-brown color or spray with gold glitter paint. You can also paint on a thin layer of glue and sprinkle it with craft sand.

6. Allow the pyramid to fully dry overnight.

Note: If you want to make a smaller pyramid, start with a 5-cube by 5-cube base.

THE GREAT PYRAMID OF GIZA

THE GREAT PYRAMID, or the Pyramid of Khufu, is the tallest pyramid. It was built for King Khufu. It is one of a group of three large pyramids at the site of Giza. The other two were built for the pharaohs Khafre and Menkaure. It is one of the Seven Wonders of the Ancient World—and the only one still standing.

How large is the Great Pyramid?

It was 481 feet (146.5 meters) tall when it was built—that's about as tall as eleven brachiosauruses. It covers 13.6 acres, which is the same size as 100 basketball courts!

How long did it take to build?

It took between 20,000 and 100,000 workers over twenty years to build!

Who designed it?

It's not known, but Hemiunu, the pharaoh's nephew, supervised its construction.

How many limestone blocks were used?

More than 2.3 million!

How did the architects get the pyramid lined up with true north?

Egyptologists think they used the stars to do this.

KHUFU'S SHIP

IN 1954, a huge boat was discovered buried deep in a stone pit beside Khufu's pyramid. It was probably put there for the pharaoh to sail across the sun with the god Ra in the afterlife. The ship was found in 1,224 separate pieces—without any instructions for putting it back together! It took archaeologists ten years to rebuild the royal boat. No nails were used—everything had been designed to fit together like puzzle pieces. The ship is 144 feet (43.89 meters) long (that's about the size of four school buses in a row) and has twelve wooden oars. A second ship was found in a separate grave nearby, but that one has not been put back together.

Were Khufu's wives buried here, too?

No. Several smaller pyramids—called Queen's Pyramids—were built nearby for his wives.

THE GREAT SPHINX

THE ANCIENT EGYPTIANS built sphinxes to guard tombs and temples. A sphinx is a mythical creature with the head of a pharaoh and the body of a lion. There are many sphinx statues throughout Egypt, but the most famous is the Great Sphinx of Giza. It's the largest and one of the oldest single-stone (that means it was carved out of one stone) statues in the world. The Great Sphinx watches over the Great Pyramids of Giza, specifically the Pyramid of Khafre.

No writings or drawings have been found on the Great Sphinx, so while Egyptologists believe King Khafre had it carved, they don't know for sure if it is an image of his face.

Its **NOSE** is missing. Egyptologists don't know what happened to it.

It wore a pharaoh's **HEADDRESS**.

It was carved out of **LIMESTONE**.

The **STONE BEARD** is missing. Pieces of the beard are on display at the British Museum in London, England.

The **TAIL** of the lion wraps around the right paw.

The **DREAM STELA**, an upright stone with the story of Prince Thutmose carved on it, also rests between its paws.

GREAT SPHINX FACTS

It measures 66 feet/20 meters tall (the same height as about three giraffes stacked on top of one another) and 240 feet/73 meters long (as long as four bowling lanes).

It was built more than 4,500 years ago.

It is located in Giza, Egypt, on the west bank of the Nile River.

It faces east, the direction of the rising sun.

It may have been built to guard the Pyramid of Khafre.

Archaeologists believe the face and body were once painted red, blue, and yellow.

Tunnels have been discovered inside, but they all stop in dead ends.

THE PRINCE'S DREAM

ONE DAY, YOUNG Prince Thutmose went out hunting. After a while, he grew tired. He spotted the Great Sphinx in the desert. The statue was buried up to its chin in the sand. The prince lay down between its paws and soon fell asleep. In his dream, the Sphinx spoke to him. The Sphinx promised to make him the next king of Egypt, but only if he could free him from the sand. The prince cleared away all the sand—and eventually became pharaoh.

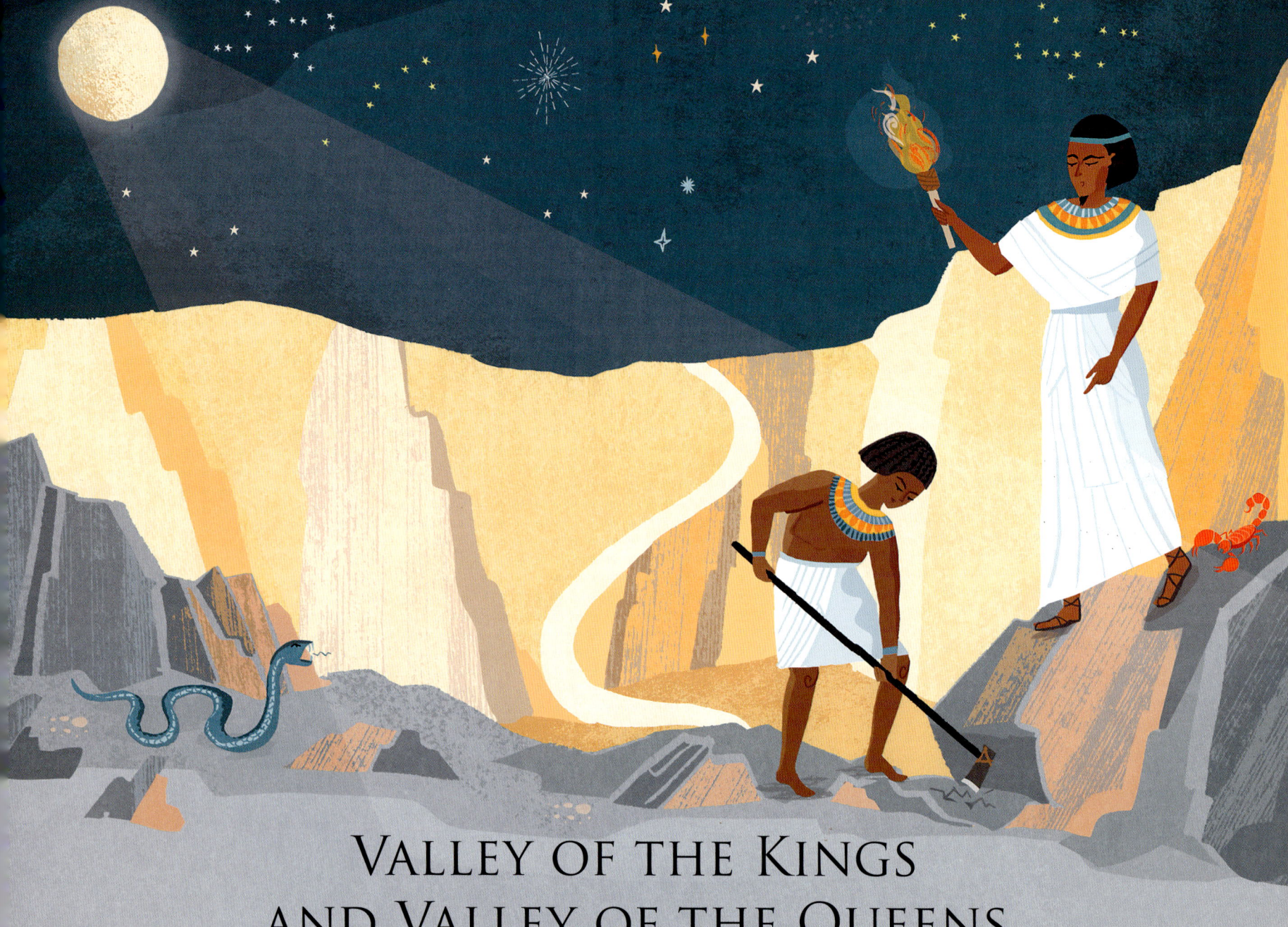

VALLEY OF THE KINGS
AND VALLEY OF THE QUEENS

A NEW PLAN

For about 1,000 years, pharaohs built enormous pyramids that rose into the sky. But the pyramids kept getting robbed. Without their treasure, the pharaohs would end up poor in the afterlife—and they definitely didn't want that! The pharaohs realized that placing a huge pyramid in the flat desert was the same as putting up a giant billboard that read: "Treasure inside! Come steal it!"

King Thutmose I decided to get tricky and build his burial site in a far-off desert location with rocky cliffs to the west of the Nile River. He secretly had his tomb cut deep into the cliffs. The pharaohs after him did the same thing. Workers had to begin building as soon as a new pharaoh was crowned king, because it took many, many years to cut these elaborate underground tombs out of the rock. When the pharaoh died, his mummified body and all his treasures were brought by boat and sled to the tomb.

This huge area of secret tombs is called the Valley of the Kings. More than sixty tombs have been discovered here so far—including those of pharaohs Tutankhamun, Seti I, and Ramses II—making it one of the world's richest archaeological sites. Egyptologists gave each tomb a number based on when it was discovered. The letters KV (King's Valley) are written before each number. So the first tomb discovered was called KV-1 and the second was KV-2, and so on.

QV-66: THE TOMB OF NEFERTARI

NOT ALL PHARAOHS

Egyptologists believe there are still undiscovered tombs, including the tombs of King Ramses VIII and King Thutmose II. But not every tomb was built for royalty. There are tombs for people who served the pharaoh and even one for the non-royal parents of a queen.

VALLEY OF THE QUEENS

The Valley of the Queens is next to the Valley of the Kings. This is where royal wives and children were buried. King Ramses I is credited with starting it. The Valley of the Queens is smaller in size than the Valley of the Kings, but more than ninety tombs have been discovered here. And there's still more digging to do, because many queens' tombs have yet to be found.

QV-66 is the tomb of Nefertari, the wife of King Ramses II. It is famous for having the most beautiful wall art and decorations.

STEP INSIDE A TOMB

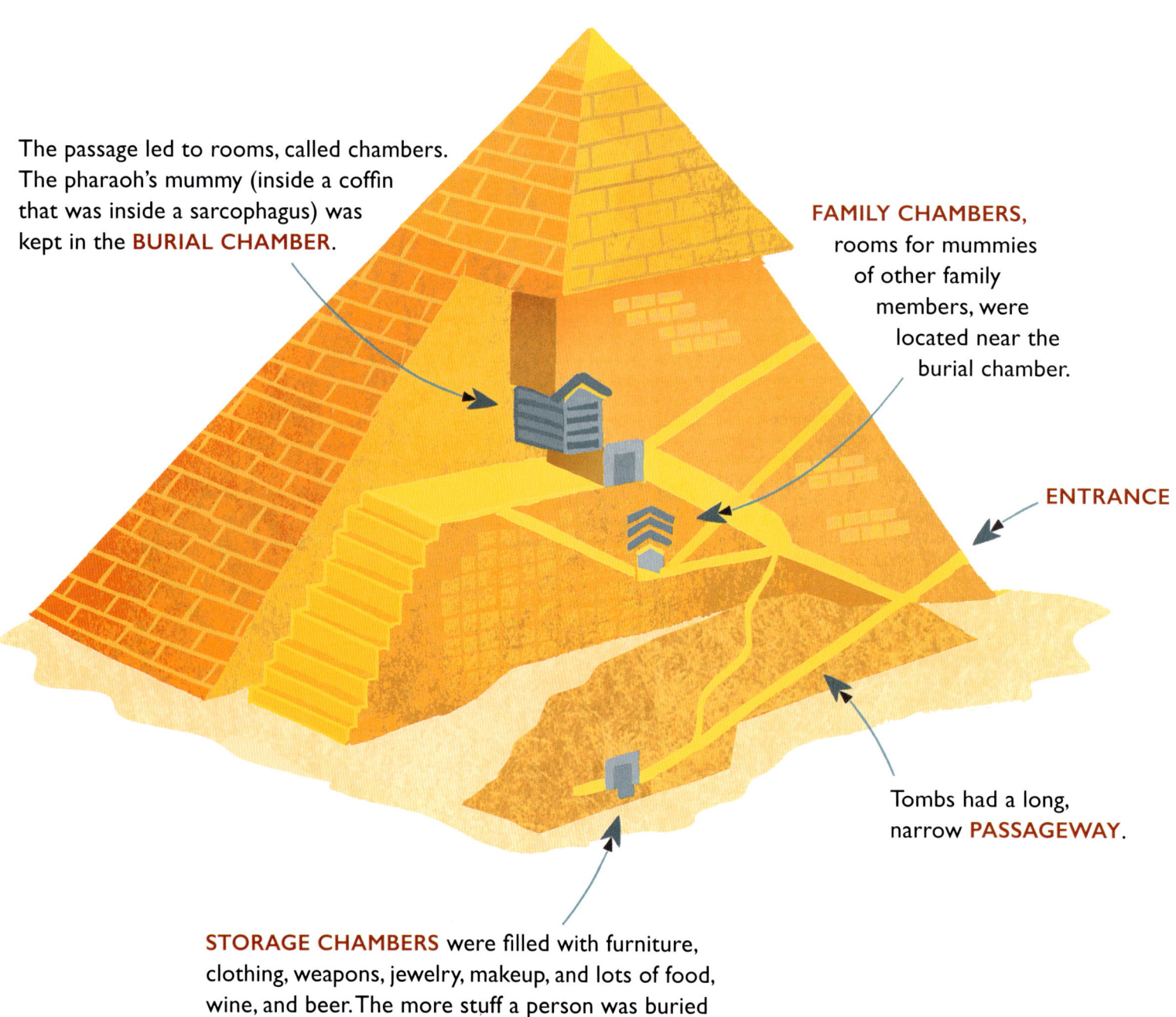

The passage led to rooms, called chambers. The pharaoh's mummy (inside a coffin that was inside a sarcophagus) was kept in the **BURIAL CHAMBER**.

FAMILY CHAMBERS, rooms for mummies of other family members, were located near the burial chamber.

ENTRANCE

Tombs had a long, narrow **PASSAGEWAY**.

STORAGE CHAMBERS were filled with furniture, clothing, weapons, jewelry, makeup, and lots of food, wine, and beer. The more stuff a person was buried with, the more he'd have in the afterlife.

THE FOOD TABLE

Plenty of food was left inside the tomb, but the dead's family was expected to continue to bring their loved one's favorite foods and drinks to the tomb and leave them on a special table. This showed the gods that the dead person was remembered and loved. The dead would "eat" the food, then return to the afterlife.

HELPING HANDS

There was still work to be done in the afterlife, so the dead were buried with shabtis, small statuettes of themselves. They were made from wood or stone and shaped like little mummies. A spell from the Book of the Dead was inscribed on the back of the shabti. If the dead person was asked in the afterlife to do manual labor, the spell would be activated, and the shabti would come to life to do it.

Royals and wealthy folks, used to being waited on by servants in life, wanted servants in the afterlife, too. So they had shabti servants buried with them, representing their servants. Pharaohs wanted *a lot* of helpers in the afterlife. One thousand shabtis were discovered in one pharaoh's tomb. Other pharaohs had 365 shabtis—one for every day of the year!

AMULETS

All ancient Egyptians—rich and poor—carried or wore amulets, or little good-luck charms. They believed amulets had magical powers to protect them from evil, heal them from sickness, and keep them healthy in life. In death, amulets with special spells were tucked into a mummy's bandages for protection during the journey through the Underworld to the afterlife.

Amulets were made from all different kinds of materials, including stone, wood, gems, gold, silver, and copper. Many were crafted from faience, a blue-green or turquoise ceramic that came from crushed sand or quartz and was thought to be magical.

Most amulets were shaped like gods, animals, or symbols.

FROG—symbol of rebirth

BABOON—symbol of wisdom

WEDJAT EYE (the Eye of Horus)—
symbol of healing and health

KNOT OF ISIS—symbol of
the power and strength of Isis

SCARAB—symbol of the
heart, renewal, and rebirth

FALCON—symbol of
the pharaoh

CROCODILE—symbol of
strength and power

Salt Dough Amulet

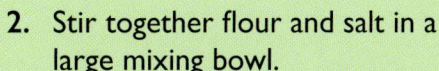

WHAT YOU NEED

- 2 cups all-purpose flour (you can substitute gluten-free flour)
- I cup salt
- I cup water
- Acrylic paint (gold, red, blue, and black)
- String or cord
- Pencil or straw

WHAT YOU DO

1. Preheat oven to 200° Fahrenheit (93° Celsius). Have an adult help you with the oven.

2. Stir together flour and salt in a large mixing bowl.

3. While stirring, gradually add the water. Mix to form a dough.

4. Roll the dough into a ball and knead for 5–10 minutes until the dough is smooth. If the dough is too sticky, add a bit more flour, or if it's too dry, add a little water.

5. Shape a small piece of the dough into your amulet. Poke a hole on top with a pencil or a straw.

6. Place the dough amulet on a baking sheet and bake for about 2 hours. (Times will vary based on the thickness of the amulet. If it's still doughy, cook it longer.)

7. Let the amulet dry completely, then paint it.

8. When the paint is dry, thread the string or cord through the hole to wear your amulet around your neck.

ANKH—symbol of life

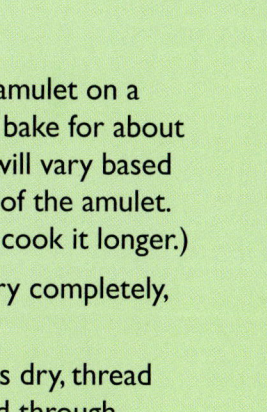

Unused dough can be stored in an airtight container in the refrigerator for up to a week. You can make a cartouche with salt dough, too!

BRIGHT AND BOLD

Bright paint was used, especially the
colors blue, black, red, and green.
Paint was made by grinding up
minerals found deep underground
and combining them with other
natural ingredients, such as egg
whites and wood gum.

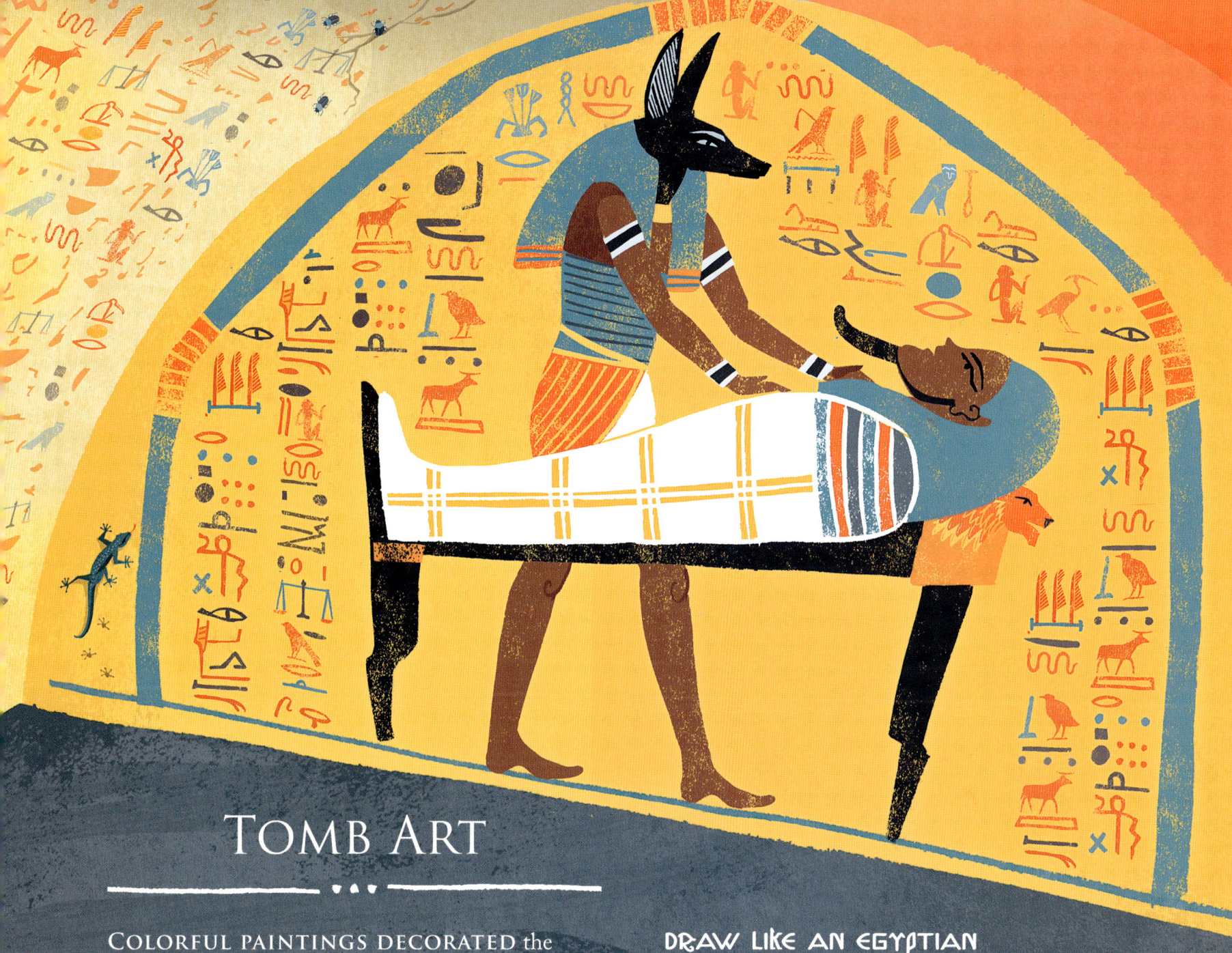

TOMB ART

COLORFUL PAINTINGS DECORATED the walls of tombs. They were painted to tell stories and to give information to both the gods and the dead. Most paintings showed scenes of daily life: harvesting fields, fishing, building boats, and preparing food.

Some later royal tombs had paintings that mapped out the route to the afterlife and included spells from the Book of the Dead.

DRAW LIKE AN EGYPTIAN

People were painted with their bodies and one eye facing forward but their heads and legs facing to the side. (Just try standing like that!) Grids were drawn on the walls (they looked like graph paper) to make sure everything lined up.

FINDING KING TUT

THE TOMB AND mummy of King Tutankhamun, also known as King Tut, were the biggest ancient Egyptian discoveries ever. King Tut's tomb was the only tomb found mostly untouched (robbers had been there twice after he was buried, but only took oils, perfumes, and some jewelry).

Here's the story…

THE RUMOR

By the early 1900s, Egyptologists believed the tombs of all the pharaohs had been found. Most had been robbed thousands of years before being discovered, leaving behind empty rooms and empty coffins.

But people often whispered about buried treasure in the desert. Some folks thought it was just a wishful story, but others were sure it was true. Egyptologists knew King Tut had been buried in the Valley of the Kings. But the boy king's tomb had never been found. Was that where the treasure was?

ENTER HOWARD CARTER

Howard Carter was born in England in 1874, and his father was an artist. He visited Egypt for the first time when he was seventeen years old. To make money, he painted pictures of the famous monuments and sold them. He soon became an archaeologist. Carter couldn't stop thinking about the stories of buried treasure in the desert. He believed King Tut's tomb was still out there—somewhere. He wanted to be the one to find it!

He decided to search the Valley of the Kings. A big expedition like this needed a lot of supplies and a lot of people—and that meant Howard Carter needed *a lot* of money. In 1907, a wealthy Englishman named Lord Carnarvon agreed to pay for the dig. Carter focused his search on one low-lying area in the valley. He had a good feeling that was where King Tut was buried. He'd found small signs—a cup and a piece of gold foil with King Tut's name on it. Carter wondered if a flood might have once pushed the sand and blocked the tomb's entrance.

Years passed without him finding anything. Other archaeologists thought he was looking in the wrong place. Carter didn't agree. He kept digging. Then he made a big discovery: the ruins of workers' huts. The tomb had to be somewhere nearby. But where?

After Carter and his crew searched the Valley of the Kings for six years, Lord Carnarvon started to run out of money and patience. He decided it was time to call it quits. Carter begged to be allowed to continue. Lord Carnarvon gave him just one last season to dig—then it would be over. The clock was ticking for Howard Carter.

THE WATER BOY

Carter hired a young boy named Hussein Abdel-Rassoul to bring the workers jars of water every day. On November 4, 1922, the boy was digging holes to rest the jars in so they wouldn't topple over, when he uncovered a step!

Then Carter found another step. And another. It was a staircase—and it led to a door!

"Open it!" the crew cried. Carter was bursting to see what was behind the secret door, but he decided it was only right to have Lord Carnarvon there, too. Lord Carnarvon was far away in England, and it took him two weeks to arrive by boat. But Carter waited.

Finally, together they brushed the rubble from the door. They saw the seal of King Tutankhamun. It was the tomb of King Tut! The door looked as if it had once been damaged, then fixed. Had robbers been here? Had they taken everything?

They opened the door and discovered a tunnel leading to a second door. Carter drilled a hole in that door. He held up a candle…

"Can you see any-thing?" asked Lord Carnarvon.

"Yes, wonderful things!" exclaimed Carter.

He saw gold everywhere! The boy king's tomb was filled with more than 5,000 priceless treasures!

FINDING TUT

Carter walked through the antechamber and entered the burial chamber. When he finally saw the big stone sarcophagus, he opened it and found a mummy case inside. He opened the mummy case…and found another mummy case. Inside the second mummy case was a third mummy case. This one was made of solid gold and inlaid with enamel and semiprecious stones in the image of the boy king. Carter opened the case—and saw King Tut's mummified body. He had been lying there untouched for more than 3,000 years.

SMALL TOMB, BIG TREASURE

As far as pharaoh's tombs went, King Tut's tomb was small. It only had four rooms. Why so small? Even though most people back then didn't live past age forty, King Tut died extremely young. Any tomb he would have started building wouldn't have been finished when he died. This tomb was probably meant for someone else.

There were the four rooms:

BURIAL CHAMBER—The sarcophagus, King Tut's mummy

TREASURY—Canopic jars (containing his organs), a gold crown, paintings, model boats, a golden throne, a cobra, his sandals, and big trunks

ANTECHAMBER—Three funeral beds, pieces from six chariots

ANNEX—Oils, dishes, board games, and other items

FUN FACT

King Tut's treasures are now in museums, but his body was left to rest in the burial chamber.

SOME OF KING TUT'S TOMB TREASURES

☑ solid gold mummy mask

☑ 6 disassembled chariots

☑ 2 full sets of senet (Senet was a popular board game. Players moved 5 disks and 5 cone pieces across a board. And 4 sticks, each with a flat and a rounded end, were used as dice.)

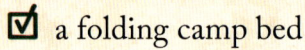

☑ 139 ivory, silver, and gold walking sticks

☑ daggers, bows, shields, and other weapons

☑ baskets filled with barley, grapes, dates, melons, and other food

☑ 48 boxes of "meat mummies"

☑ a pair of sandals that had paintings of his enemies on the soles, letting him "crush" them with every step he took

☑ a leopard-skin cloak

☑ a folding camp bed

☑ musical instruments

☑ solid gold fans and ostrich-feather fans

☑ a makeup kit

☑ headrests to prop up his neck while sleeping

☑ 2 trumpets

☑ clean underwear

THE MUMMY'S CURSE

THE OPENING OF King Tut's tomb caused huge excitement all over the world. Every newspaper and magazine wrote stories about the discoveries—and about the mummy's curse that would be unleashed on anyone who dared to disturb the boy king's tomb.

In the years that followed, the press reported some strange events:

- Lord Carnarvon died from an infected mosquito bite five months after the tomb was opened. His dog, back in England, died the same day as he did.

- Lord Carnarvon's pet canary, which he'd brought to Egypt with him, was supposedly killed by a cobra.

- Howard Carter gave one of his friends a paper-weight made from a mummified hand, and then his friend's house burned down.

- A rich American who'd visited the tomb died of pneumonia.

- A technician who x-rayed the mummy died of a mysterious illness.

Was the curse real?

No written curse was ever found in the tomb, and Howard Carter did not believe in the curse. The curse and the rumors started when the *New York World* published a letter from a popular fiction author who predicted that everyone who had been in the tomb would die from an ancient curse. Right after that, Lord Carnarvon happened to die. The press went wild. All the papers printed story after story about "The Curse of Tutankhamun." But out of forty people who'd been there when the boy king's tomb was opened, only six died within twelve years, which was not all that unusual, because several were in poor health or were elderly. And Howard Carter lived until 1939, almost twenty years after the tomb was opened.

Were there any real mummy curses?

The walls of a few early mastabas were inscribed with warnings to frighten away grave robbers. They threatened thieves with punishment by the gods and death by divine lions, crocodiles, scorpions, or snakes. But the other pyramids and tombs that have been discovered have not contained written curses.

EGYPTMANIA HITS THE WEST END

The Daily News

The Weather
FRIDAY: SUNNY WITH CHANCE OF SHOWERS

FRIDAY, APRIL 6, 1923 - FORTY EIGHT PAGES.   TWO CENTS   VOLUME 147 ISSUE 44

CURSE OF PHARAOHS UNLEASHED

Tomb Digging to Go On Despite Curse of Egypt

TOMB ROBBERS

SPARKLING JEWELRY, PRECIOUS gems, shiny amulets, and gold mummy cases were just some of the incredible riches buried in pyramids and tombs. They were meant to travel with the dead into the afterlife, but many never made it. What happened?

Thieves—also called tomb robbers—broke in and stole the treasures. Sometimes they stole mummies, too, to get the gold and silver amulets wrapped up inside. Guards watched the pyramids day and night, yet still robbers found their way in. Every pyramid discovered in Egypt had been robbed at some point.

KA-CHING!

King Tut was just a boy when he died, yet the value of the loot found inside his small tomb is worth around three-quarters of a billion dollars today! Imagine how much the treasure buried in the enormous tombs and pyramids of longtime pharaohs Ramses II and Khufu would have been worth!

WHICH WAY?

Tomb robbers didn't always have an easy time finding the loot. The way the insides of many pyramids and tombs were designed for religious and symbolic reasons ended up making getting in and out confusing. There were:

• Long, narrow passages arranged in a maze

• Dead ends and fake passages that led nowhere

• Fake burial chambers, with the real burial chambers placed far away from the main entrance

• A false main entrance, with the real entrance hidden behind stone slabs or tons of rubble

But, often, thieves were able to chisel through the rock, tunnel through walls, and find hidden rooms of treasure. (Or, sometimes, they may have paid a dishonest guard to let them in!)

CRIME AND PUNISHMENT

Tomb robbers were punished harshly when caught. The soles of their feet were beaten with a rod, and often they were killed.

DESTROYING MUMMIES

FOR MANY YEARS, people didn't understand that the mummies were as valuable as the treasure buried with them. Sometimes, when tombs were opened, mummies were thrown away. Foreigners visiting Egypt brought mummies home as souvenirs of their trip. Mummies were sold to universities, pharmacies, and art collectors. It took a long time for the Egyptian government and scientists to educate people that mummies should be respected and treated as priceless artifacts important to history and science.

MUMMIES AS PARTY ENTERTAINMENT

In the early to mid-1800s, fashionable people in London, Paris, and New York brought back mummies from trips to Egypt and had unwrapping parties in their homes. Guests came to watch the mummy being unwrapped and see what amulets—or "treasures"—they'd find inside. Food and drinks were served. Musicians played. Sometimes a professor lectured. But unwrapping caused the mummies to disintegrate after they came in contact with moist air. Historians have no idea how many mummies were destroyed (and amulets lost) by unwrapping parties.

MUMMIES AS HEALTH FOOD

For hundreds of years, people didn't understand how mummification worked. They falsely believed that mummies contained magic and that this let them stay lifelike for eternity. So they ate ground-up mummy, hoping to become stronger and more powerful. And they plastered ground-up mummy over injuries and tumors, hoping they'd heal. In the 1500s, France's King Francis II ate a pinch of mummy every day. In the 1600s, England's King Charles II collected mummies and rubbed the dust from them onto his skin to "absorb" their greatness. And up until 1920, pharmacies sold mummy powder as medicine.

MUMMIES AS PAINT

Starting around the 1500s, ground-up mummy was used to make paint in Europe. They called the color "mummy brown." It was a very popular color—until artists found out how it was created!

MUMMY RESPECT

For centuries, mummies were seen as objects and not as people. Today mummies are kept safe in temperature-controlled museums. It is against the law to take them out of Egypt. They're no longer unwrapped but instead are scanned with digital technology to learn about the past.

What Happened to Ancient Egypt?

After Cleopatra's death, the Romans conquered Egypt. Egypt became a part of the Roman Empire, and that ended almost 3,000 years of Egyptian rule. In 1882, Egypt was occupied and controlled by the British. This lasted until 1953, when Egypt finally gained its independence and became the Republic of Egypt.

EGYPTOMANIA

French general Napoleon Bonaparte brought his army to Egypt in 1798 and returned with stories of pyramids, mummies, and the wonders he found. This started "Egyptomania"—a craze in Europe for everything Egyptian. England and France sent competing teams of archaeologists to hunt for tombs and

treasure. Howard Carter discovered King Tut's tomb in 1922, and the whole world once again became fascinated. Today you can see mummies, art, sculpture, and other ancient Egyptian artifacts in museums all over the world.

But over the last few decades, Egypt has been working to have many of these treasures returned to their ancient homeland—the land of the mighty Nile River, fertile soil, desert sands, powerful pharaohs, magical gods, and an amazing, inventive people.

Museums to View Mummies and Ancient Egyptian Art

AFRICA

- Egyptian Museum, Cairo, Egypt
- Grand Egyptian Museum, Giza, Egypt
- Luxor Museum, Luxor, Egypt
- Nubian Museum, Aswan, Egypt

AUSTRALIA

- The Australian Museum, Sydney, Australia

EUROPE

- British Museum, London, United Kingdom
- Louvre Museum, Paris, France
- Museo Egizio, Turin, Italy
- National Museums Scotland, Edinburgh, Scotland
- Neues Museum, Berlin, Germany
- Petrie Museum, London, England

NORTH AMERICA

- Brooklyn Museum, Brooklyn, New York
- Denver Museum of Nature and Science, Denver, Colorado
- Hearst Museum of Anthropology, Berkeley, California
- Kelsey Museum of Archeology, Ann Arbor, Michigan
- Metropolitan Museum of Art, New York, New York
- Museum of Fine Arts, Boston, Massachusetts
- The Oriental Institute at the University of Chicago, Chicago, Illinois
- Royal Ontario Museum, Toronto, Ontario, Canada
- Smithsonian National Museum of Natural History, Washington, D.C.
- University of Pennsylvania Museum of Archaeology and Anthropology, Philadelphia, Pennsylvania

Pronunciation Guide

Akhenaten: a-KUH-nah-ton

Akhet: ah-KET

Amenhotep: ah-men-HOE-tep

Ammit: AM-it

amulet: AM-u-let

Amun: AM-un

ankh: AHNK

Anubis: a-NOO-bis

Apep: ah-PEP

ba: BAH

Bastet: BAST

Bes: BES

Caesar: SEE-zr

canopic: can-OH-pick

cartouche: car-TOOSH

Cleopatra: KLEE-oh-PAT-rah

demotic: dih-MOT-ik

Djoser: ZO-ser

Duamutef: DO-mew-tef

Duat: DO-aht

Egyptologist: EE-jip-TOL-uh-jist

Geb: JHEB

Giza: GEE-za

Hapy: HAH-pee

Hathor: HATH-or

Hatshepsut: hat-SHEP-sut

Hemiunu: HIM-ew-new

hieroglyph: HY-ro-GLIF

Horus: HOR-us

Imhotep: im-HO-tep

Imsety: im-SET-ee

Isis: EYE-sis

ka: KAH

Khafre: KAH-fray

Khepri: KHEP-ree

Khufu: KOO-foo

Ma'at: MAH-at

mastaba: MAS-tuh-buh

muu: MOO

myrrh: MUR

natron: NAY-tron

Nefertari: NEF-er-TARE-ee

Nefertiti: NEF-er-TEE-tee

nemes: NEE-ms

Nephthys: NEP-these

Nut: NUT

Octavian: oc-TAY-vee-un

Osiris: oh-SIRE-is

papyrus: puh-PIE-rus

Peret: PAIR-it

pharaoh: FARE-oh

Ptolemy: TOL-e-mee

Qebehsenuef: keb-SEN-oo-if

Ra: RAH

Ramses: RAM-sees

sarcophagus: sar-KAHF-uh-gus

scarab: SCARE-ab

Sekhmet: SEK-met

Seth: SET

shabti: SHAHB-tee

Shemu: SHEH-moo

Shu: SHOE

Sobek: SO-beck

sphinx: SFINKS

Taweret: Ta-WER-et

Tefnut: TEF-noot

Thoth: TOT

Thutmose: TUT-moz

Tutankhamun:
    TOOT-ahn-KAH-mun

Tutankhaten:
    TOOT-ahn-KAH-ten

uraeus: you-REE-us

wedjat: WID-jet

INDEX

ENJOY THE REST OF THE CHILD'S INTRODUCTION SERIES!

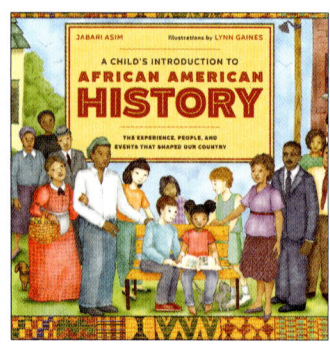

A Child's Introduction to African American History

A Child's Introduction to Art

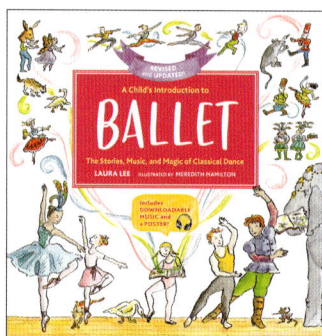

A Child's Introduction to Ballet

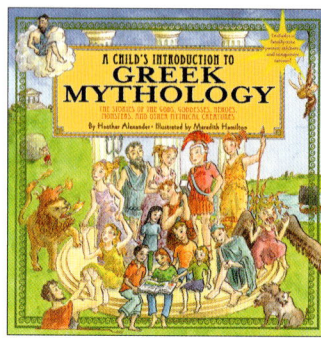

A Child's Introduction to Greek Mythology

A Child's Introduction to the Environment

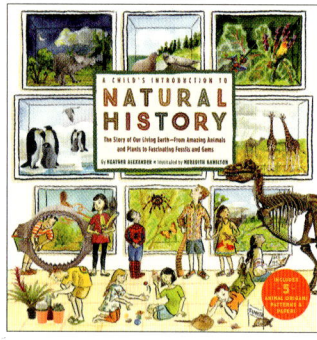

A Child's Introduction to Natural History

A Child's Introduction to the Night Sky

A Child's Introduction to Norse Mythology

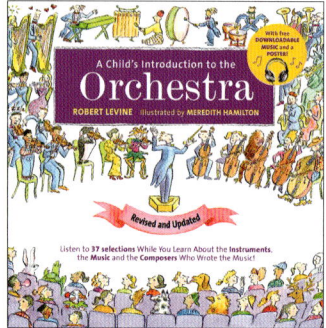

A Child's Introduction to the Orchestra

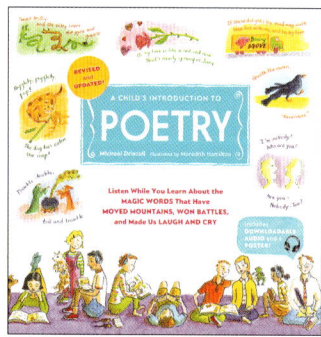

A Child's Introduction to Poetry

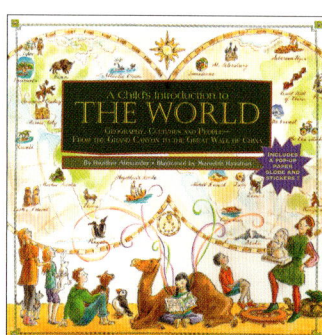

A Child's Introduction to the World